Walking through the Wardrobe

A Devotional Quest into
The Lion, the Witch and the Wardrobe

WALKING

WARI

THROUGH THE
ΟROBE

A DEVOTIONAL QUEST INTO *The Lion, the Witch and the Wardrobe*

SARAH ARTHUR

Tyndale House Publishers, Inc., Wheaton, Illinois

Go to areUthirsty.com for the latest

Visit www.saraharthur.com to learn more about Sarah Arthur

TYNDALE is a registered trademark of Tyndale House Publishers, Inc.

thirsty[?] and the *thirsty[?]* logo are trademarks of Tyndale House Publishers, Inc.

The Lion, the Witch and the Wardrobe is a trademark of C. S. Lewis (Pte) Ltd.

Walking through the Wardrobe

Library of Congress Cataloging-in-Publication Data

Arthur, Sarah.
  Walking through the wardrobe : a devotional quest into The lion, the witch, and the wardrobe / Sarah Arthur.
      p. cm.
  Includes bibliographical references.
  ISBN-13: 978-1-4143-0766-4
  ISBN-10: 1-4143-0766-7
  I. Lewis, C. S. (Clive Staples), 1898—1963. Lion, the witch, and the wardrobe.
2. Children's stories, English—History and criticism.   3. Christian fiction, English—History and criticism.   4. Fantasy fiction, English—History and criticism.   5. Quests (Expeditions) in literature.   6. Narnia (Imaginary place)
I. Title.

Printed in the United States of America

II	10	09	08	07	06	05
7	6	5	4	3	2	I

For my parents,
who gave me the keys to the Kingdom

WHAT'S INSIDE

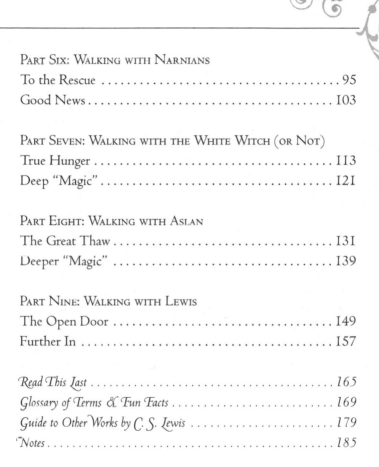

A NOTE FROM THE AUTHOR

I must have been in fourth or fifth grade when I decided
to write a letter to Macmillan Publishers, asking if they
would please send me the address of an author by the
name of C. S. Lewis. There were some burning questions
I wanted to ask him about Narnia; namely, was he plan-
ning to write more than seven books? I was under-
standably stricken to receive a reply that read something
like this (I've since misplaced the original):

> DEAR MS. FAULMAN,
>
> Thank you for your letter requesting information
> on C. S. Lewis. We regret to inform you that Mr.
> Lewis died in 1963. However, he wrote a great
> many other works that you might enjoy someday,
> including [*insert boring grown-up stuff about literary criti-
> cism, Christian apologetics, satire, science fiction, etc.*]. Have a
> nice day.
>
> SINCERELY,
> *People Who Have No Clue They Just Crushed Your Little Heart*

I'm sure their intentions were good, but to a kid in love with Narnia, it was like being told you just had your last birthday and there won't be another one again, ever. You blew out your last candle. No more presents. And not only that, but Christmas is canceled too.

Needless to say, it was my last letter to a publishing company for a long time. But I kept reading the Narnia stories, over and over again, savoring every morsel, knowing there wouldn't be any more on the plate when I was done. I read those stories throughout middle school and on into high school too. I specifically remember the day when a fellow student in my ninth grade history class noticed *The Magician's Nephew* on my desk and said, "You know those books are, like, spiritual and stuff, right? You know that Lewis was a Christian?"

The funny thing is, I'd never once considered that C. S. Lewis might have *intentionally* put Christian symbolism in the books. No one had handed me the Secret Decoder Ring and said, "You know that Aslan is supposed to be Jesus, right?" Okay, so I was a little dense. Or maybe (as I like to think) I had a greater level of appreciation for the stories because I wasn't jaded and cynical, always looking for the hidden agenda behind a work of art.

Whatever the case, I look back on that moment in my history class as, well, historical. It changed the entire way I read the Narnia books. In fact, it sent me reading them all over again, this time more attuned to the powerful spiritual and biblical parallels woven throughout the pages. But more important, it gave me an even greater interest in the man named C. S. Lewis. By the time I was a senior, I was ready to explore who this guy was. What did he believe? What other stuff had he written? How did a believer like him write such excellent, smart, powerful fiction and not water it down with cheesy, sloppy "Christianity lite"?

Right. So I'd become a *bit* more jaded and cynical by that time. But not about Lewis. Here was a spiritual varsity coach, the kind who could kick my lazy butt when it came to living the Christian life. I decided to do my senior literature paper on three of his other works: *The Screwtape Letters*, *Mere Christianity*, and his autobiography, *Surprised by Joy*. Even though there'd never be another

Narnia book from the pen of arguably the greatest children's writer of the twentieth century, there were plenty of other works by Lewis to keep me occupied for the rest of my life.

Fifteen years later, I'm still reading Lewis, still cracking open the covers of *The Lion, the Witch and the Wardrobe* on a yearly basis to experience that magical world all over again, often discovering things I'd never noticed before. And now that *The Lord of the Rings* wizards at Weta Workshop in New Zealand are teaming up with Andrew Adamson, Disney, and Walden Media in bringing Narnia to life on the big screen, I'm sure I'll discover even more.

So the "magic" of C. S. Lewis never really ends, as some of my friends have said. We just continue to walk further in, through the wardrobe, past our initial childhood interest in the world of Narnia, and into the spiritual themes that shaped the life and works of a beloved author. In fact, the adventure has only just begun!

Sarah Faulman Arthur

ACKNOWLEDGMENTS

My heartfelt thanks to the following people, whose encouragement and wisdom contributed, directly and indirectly, to the creation of this book: Jan Axford, Erin Keeley Marshall, David and Teresa Crouse, Chris Mitchell, Chip Duncan, Dabney Hart, Rolland Hein, and Kent Gramm. Also to my writing buddies of all stripes, including Jenna Mindel, Kathy Paterka, Karen LaCross, Kris Rasmussen, Jami Blaauw-Hara, and the erstwhile 45th Parallel Writer's Group. And to the members of the Northern Michigan C. S. Lewis Festival board; the Mythopoeic Society; my own dear family and friends; and most of all, my husband, Tom, whose spiritual thaw began in part while reading *The Chronicles of Narnia* the year we first met.

> *When I think of all this, I fall to my knees and pray*
> *to the Father.*
> EPHESIANS 3:14

READ THIS FIRST

It has been almost two whole years, but you and your Weta-geek friends are finally back in action, standing in line before Christmas for yet another long-awaited midnight movie premiere. In front of you is a *LOTR* junkie who looks about *this close* to flunking out of grad school, and behind you is a pip-squeak of a third grader whose dad looks about *this close* to dragging him back home:

"I thought this was *The Polar Express*."

"Nope. That was last year, Dad."

"So what is it?"

"Duh! It's Narnia. Sheesh."

"Narnia. What's that? Sounds Elvish or something. Wait—is this one of those *Lord of the Flies* movies?"

"*Lord of the Rings*."

"Right. Anyway, what's it rated? If it's got all those crazy creatures and battle scenes and stuff, we're going home."

Meanwhile, the *LOTR* junkie in front of you is muttering into his cell phone, "Dude, take the left aisle, row fifteen from the back. I'll be there as quick as I can. No, I'm in line; I somehow got stuck in Barneyland. Seriously, the little kid behind me is, like, *two years old*. He'll be crying like a baby when they open the doors. Don't his parents have a clue?"

Clearly not, you realize, after a few more minutes of eavesdropping. You and your Weta-geek friends exchange smug looks. You almost feel sorry for the dad. Because the minute those doors open, the battle for Middle-earth has nothing on the theater lobby, and Pip-squeak had better make a run for the car.

Yep, the New Zealand crew who created the big-screen *LOTR* trilogy is back for another blockbuster, but this time with C. S. Lewis's *Chronicles of Narnia*. If all goes well, *The Lion, the Witch and the Wardrobe* will be only the first in a series, and from now on we won't go for more than a few years at a time without the magic of the wizards at Weta Workshop taking the New Zealand landscape by storm and our breath away. After three solid years of *The Lord of the Rings* hype, we're looking for a little excitement again, a bit of fantasy magic to make our lives feel like the adventure we wish they could be.

Sigh. If only life were more on the scale of Orlando Bloom taking down the giant Oliphaunt in *The Return of the King* rather than the usual, tedious mall-crawl with the Abercrombie crowd! We often wish the daily grind held a greater resemblance to all those fantasy worlds we've come to love, don't we? In our more desperate moments, we're tempted to walk smack into pillars at subway stations, just to see if we end up at Platform Nine and Three-Quarters. And which of us, at some point in our not-so-distant childhood (yes, let's be honest!), hasn't pushed aside the coats in a closet, hoping to find an entrance to another world?

The disappointing fact that most closets lead only to drywall doesn't eliminate our thirst for fantasylands: places where mystery, adventure, romance, and dangerous quests are the order of the day. Even while yawning in class or surfing the Net, we hunger for other worlds. We long to go beyond the streets we know, beyond our familiar woods and fields, and into the land of Faerie; to Middle-earth, Narnia, or Summerland; to the kingdom east of the sun and west of the moon.

This longing isn't incidental. It's something we're born with. Most of us, if we're honest, sense with unease that this world is not all there is. At times we get inner hints and glimpses of *something* beyond what the eye can see. Eventually we begin to suspect that there is another Kingdom out there, perhaps closer than we realize, possibly even just through that door.

We're not the first people to suspect such a thing. The author C. S. Lewis, long before he put pen to paper and created the magical world of Narnia, was a skeptical teenager who didn't believe in other worlds. According to *Surprised by Joy*, even though he loved all the old fantasy tales about kings and battles and epic adventures, he was intellectually opposed to the concept of an actual spiritual world beyond what science can prove. He was officially an atheist who especially didn't want to believe in some God in heaven who would hold us accountable for the stuff we do on earth. Christianity, in his opinion, was just another myth—one that only simple, uneducated people are foolish enough to believe.

Yet his imagination longed for something more. He was in his mid-teens when he picked up the fantasy book *Phantastes*, written by a Christian writer named George MacDonald. Within a few hours, Lewis realized he "had crossed a great frontier."[1] He no longer simply yearned for another world; he yearned for the "goodness" and "holiness" of that world, wherever and whatever it was.[2] Though he didn't know it at the time (and it would be a long while before he finally converted to Christianity), the good and holy world he encountered in George MacDonald's story was a reflection of the Kingdom of God itself.

The Kingdom of God. We see the phrase sprinkled throughout the pages of the New Testament, especially in the Gospels (the first four books). People sing about it in church. We hear it from the lips of Christians. But do we really know what it is? *Where* is it, exactly? Can we set out on a journey to find it? What sorts of roads do we take to get there? How do we know when we've found it?

It's a topic Jesus was especially keen on. "How can I
describe the Kingdom of God?" he asked the crowds
gathered to hear him speak. "What story should I use to
illustrate it?" (Mark 4:30). He used mysterious parables
to spark their curiosity: The Kingdom is like a farmer; it's
like a treasure hunt, like a woman working yeast into
some dough. It's like a fishing net, a mustard seed, a pearl
of great price found at a market stall. In other words, the
Kingdom is not a political coup, as Jesus' listeners were
hoping. It's not even a physical place at all—at least, not
yet. It's been here all the time, waiting to be found in the
midst of everyday life, as close as your heartbeat. Jesus
said, "The Kingdom of God is already among you"
(Luke 17:21).

What? You mean, the Kingdom isn't some magical
place you can only reach if you know the right incanta-
tions or open the right closet doors? You mean it's not
some airy-fairy heavenly realm in the clouds? Nope.
Instead, wherever God is acknowledged as Lord and King,
that's the Kingdom. Our universe itself was originally the
perfect Kingdom, ruled by the Creator who made it, but
we humans on planet Earth have been in rebellion against

the true King since the beginning of time. Then just when things were looking really hopeless, God sent his Prince, Jesus, into rebel territory to conquer evil and free us to be true citizens of the Kingdom again. We can choose to be his subjects or not—with just consequences either way. That's the essential story we find in the Bible, and it's the essential story at the heart of each of our lives.

And that's what all good fantasy stories have at their core, whether or not it's a conscious theme. J. R. R. Tolkien, author of *The Lord of the Rings*, made this case convincingly to his friend and colleague C. S. Lewis, years after Lewis's life-altering reading of *Phantastes*.[3] All fairy tales, Tolkien argued, echo the gospel of Jesus Christ in some way because the gospel is the True Story; it's the real fairy tale that crashed into the time line of history.[4] And eventually Lewis accepted Tolkien's reasoning. "The heart of Christianity is a myth which is also a fact," Lewis wrote.[5] The Kingdom we all long for, beyond the world we know, is real after all. This idea became a major theme in Lewis's writings from that point on, including—and perhaps most especially—in the land of Narnia.

It's as if God was whispering into Lewis's imagination: "How can I describe the Kingdom of God? What story should I use to illustrate it?" Even as the images of a faun in a snowy wood and a queen on her wintry sledge came unbidden to Lewis's mind, Aslan came bounding into the story as the true king of that fallen, imaginary realm. And the rest of us are drawn into a tale of high adventure where the stakes are nothing less than the rescue of a rebel for the salvation of an entire land, and the outcome is nothing greater than the crowning of the Sons and Daughters of Adam and Eve.

Someday, the Bible promises, Jesus the King will return to this physical earth, and our fallen, sinful world will be conquered once and for all: "The world has now become the Kingdom of our Lord and of his Christ, and he will reign forever and ever" (Revelation 11:15). We'll reign beside him as kings and queens (Luke 22:29-30). We'll finally have the spiritual eyes to see what's been there all along.

Meanwhile, as Christians, we walk this journey of faith with one foot in the Kingdom and one in *this* world—the ordinary, humdrum, painful, and even frightening planet we've been given as our home. The careful dance we do is that of trying to live our waking hours in this fallen place without forgetting that God's realm is our true home in the end. Our attitudes, dreams, beliefs, values, behaviors, and words are to be shaped by those of our Lord, not by those of this rebellious world. We are to live like true Narnians, so to speak, in the here and now.

And that's what we're truly longing for. On those weekends when we're suddenly gripped with the urge to watch all three extended editions of *The Lord of the Rings*, what we really want, deep down inside (besides therapy), is the assurance that there is a realm someplace where evil has been conquered once and for all. And when we hear the voice of Aslan booming through the surround sound of the darkened theater and our hearts feel a stab of joy, what we really yearn for is the voice of our true King and Savior saying, "Well done!" (Luke 19:17). We want to live like citizens of his country, even in the midst of our daily lives.

And we can.

HOW TO USE THIS BOOK

Walking through the Wardrobe is not some attempt to convince
you that God exists or that faith is relevant to our lives
today. Reading the works of C. S. Lewis or J. R. R.
Tolkien is enough to settle all those arguments at once.
Those guys believed in God. Not only that, but they
claimed Christ as Lord and King. They viewed writing
fairy tales as a God-given task: to help us readers open
our hearts to the invisible Kingdom of God through
stories that take place beyond the world we know.

So this book is meant to be a devotional guide to help
you grow in your faith. Each chapter is a short reflection
on a spiritual theme connected with *The Lion, the Witch and
the Wardrobe*, followed by questions and related Bible passages to help you go "Further In." Some thoughts to keep
in the back of your mind as you read are *How does this apply
to my everyday life?* and *What am I going to do about it?*

In preparation for reading these devotions, you'll want
to (a) familiarize yourself with the movie or the book

version of *The Lion, the Witch and the Wardrobe*; (b) grab a pen or pencil to scribble your thoughts for the "Further In" questions; and (c) have a Bible handy (we recommend the New Living Translation for this book). For those who are only recently becoming familiar with C. S. Lewis and the land of Narnia, the Glossary of Terms & Fun Facts in the back can help you keep track of people, places, and things in *The Lion, the Witch and the Wardrobe*. It also includes some fun facts that Lewis fans might not have known (such as where the word *Narnia* comes from). And finally, there's a guide to reading other works by Lewis while you wait for the next Narnia movie.

You'll notice that the eighteen devotions in this book are organized into nine pairs, each pair focusing on a particular character in *LWW*. For those who are familiar with *Walking with Frodo* and *Walking with Bilbo* (areUthirsty.com), you'll recognize a similar "walking" theme in this book too. That's because almost all the characters in the stories of C. S. Lewis and J. R. R. Tolkien are on a journey—a quest—and we have much to learn from them about our own quest for the Kingdom. In walking with them, what do we discover?

For those who are new to reading devotional books, welcome to a truly unique genre that is designed to encourage and challenge you to live what you believe. As often as you might feel like all this Christian spiritual stuff is totally hokey, something inside of you secretly longs for another world, the place you can finally call home. Like the teenage Lewis, you may not be ready to admit it yet with your mind, your heart, or even your conscience, but your imagination saw the open door to the true Kingdom long ago and began the journey further in.

Now it's time for the rest of you to follow.

Thoughts to Get You Started

- If you could walk alongside any character in any fantasy story, who would it be? Why?

- Have you ever found yourself longing for the other worlds you read about in books or watch in movies? What makes you want to go there?

- What hints or glimpses have you been given into the "otherworld" of God's Kingdom?

The Word on the Kingdom

Take some time to read one or more of the following Bible passages:

PSALM 145:10-13; MATTHEW 2:1-2; MARK 12:32-34; JOHN 18:36-37; COLOSSIANS 1:15-16; HEBREWS 12:28

PART ONE
Walking with Lucy

She's the youngest in the family but the first to find a way into Narnia. Following in her footsteps takes a dose of curiosity, a pile of courage, and a whopping amount of childlike faith. Are you game?

Never Too Old

You've heard their snide comments before. Yeah, you know who I mean: those *LOTR* junkies who sneer at people for liking the Narnia stories. "Dude, Tolkien's stuff is so much *deeper* and more *complex*," they say, punctuating the comment with some quote in Elvish. And then they add, "Narnia is for *kids*."

Oh, really? Then why was it written by a grown-up?

Tolkien himself maintained, "If fairy-story as a kind is

worth reading at all it is worthy to be written for and read by adults."[6] Lewis agreed: "It certainly is my opinion that a book worth reading only in childhood is not worth reading even then."[7] So if the Narnia stories meant anything to us when we were kids, they can still mean something now— possibly even more. We're never too old.

Check out Lewis's inscription to his goddaughter, Lucy Barfield, on the inside page of *The Lion, the Witch and the Wardrobe*. He indicated that at some point she'd probably grow out of the book, but then she'd grow into it again. In other words, we all go through a stage when we think we're too cool or too grown-up for all that "kid stuff." But then we reach a point when we've matured in humility enough that we can regain that sense of delight and wide-eyed wonder.

Even so, there will always be those who consider such behavior childish. In Lewis's day, the Oxford don was surrounded by other scholars who could act very superior and snobbish when they wanted to, which was most of the time. Anything written in plain, everyday English— especially for children—was considered beneath them. In their minds, Lewis wasn't supposed to be writing stuff like that. He was supposed to act responsible and grown-up and write scholarly works that only smart people read. (He did that too, but that's not what he became famous for.)

Along with children's books, he also wrote stuff about the Christian faith using words that ordinary people could understand. Apparently, he wasn't supposed to be doing that either (even Tolkien was fairly annoyed with him about that, especially when Lewis dedicated *The Screwtape Letters* to him[8]). But it bothered Lewis that the theologians and ministers weren't writing about God and faith in a way that the everyday person could grasp. If the theologians didn't get their act together and write at a readable level, then who would? Lewis would, that's who. Because, he insisted, *some*body had to.[9]

So, for his childlike attitude toward both fantasy and faith, Lewis was looked at askance by the academic community. Needless to say, it was a painful road. No wonder he could write so convincingly about Lucy's experience after her first journey to Narnia!

Of course, it's no accident that the youngest child in

the Pevensie family—the one who's the most curious and
open and willing—is the first to get into the otherworld.
And as a result of her simple faith, she's not only disbe-
lieved by the others, but she's picked on for insisting it's
not just a game, particularly by Edmund (who, incidentally, is trying very hard to be grown up). She's penalized
for having a childlike attitude and loses the trust of those
closest to her. Yet eventually, after their adventures in
Narnia have reached a peaceful conclusion, Lucy is called
Queen Lucy the Valiant. Apparently, childlike faith and
perseverance are attitudes Aslan honors.

They're attitudes Jesus honors too.

Frederick Buechner writes, "When Jesus is asked who is
the greatest in the kingdom of Heaven, he reaches into the
crowd and pulls out a child with a cheek full of bubble
gum and eyes full of whatever a child's eyes are full of and
says unless you can become like that, don't bother to ask."[10]

From Jesus' perspective, it takes the humility of a child
to grasp what the Kingdom is all about. Those who think
they are too grown up or cool for all that simple faith business are missing the mark. The disciples included. When a

group of parents tries to bring their children to see Jesus, the disciples shoo them away because they don't have VIP passes. But Jesus welcomes the children and says, "The Kingdom of God belongs to those who are like these children. I tell you the truth, anyone who doesn't receive the Kingdom of God like a child will never enter it" (Luke 18:16-17). Particularly those who are trying so hard to be grown up.

In one of his New Testament letters, the missionary Paul wrote, "When I was a child, I spoke and thought and reasoned as a child. But when I grew up, I put away childish things" (1 Corinthians 13:11). Note how he didn't say, "I put away child*like* things." There's a difference between the humble, child*like* faith that Jesus says we must have to enter the Kingdom and the self-centered, child*ish* attitudes that keep us from experiencing the wonder of what God has in store for us.

Plenty of adults are childish about their faith. There's nothing more ridiculously juvenile than people thinking they have to be grown up and serious when it comes to living the Christian life. Sure, there are times when we need to be serious about things like worship. Passing notes about the music leader's mullet is just plain childish. But delight and awe in the presence of God—true worship—isn't. Someone with a childlike attitude can still take faith seriously without putting on a long face and shushing everyone else.

All our attempts to be grown up and cool are really just evidence of childish selfishness anyway. We don't want our pride to be hurt. We don't want to earn the disrespect of our peers. We don't want to be picked on for being shallow or simple. So we cop an attitude of cool and hope it passes for smart. But it's probably time to shake the whole "I'm too cool for that" demeanor and follow Lucy into the wardrobe. Otherwise, we'll never reach the Kingdom at all.

Entering the Kingdom requires childlike faith. What will it take for you to be a kid again?

I tell you the truth, unless you turn from your sins and become like little children, you will never get into the Kingdom of Heaven.

MATTHEW 18:3

Further In

• What attitudes, habits, or enjoyments should you hang on to from childhood, and what should you grow out of? Why?

• Why is childlikeness an important quality in the Kingdom of God?

• What are some child*ish* attitudes that come between you and your ability to take delight in what God is doing in your life?

• How willing are you to be a kid again when it comes to trusting in Jesus? What holds you back?

• What are you going to do about it?

The Word on Childlike Faith

Take some time to read one or more of the following Bible passages:

ISAIAH 11:6; MATTHEW 11:25; MARK 9:36-37; ROMANS 8:15-17; 2 TIMOTHY 3:14-15; 1 JOHN 3:1-2

Come and See

"COME AND SEE," Lucy says to her siblings when words fail her to describe the magical land she's discovered through the wardrobe (chapter 3). And curiously enough, even though her brothers and sister sincerely believe it's impossible for there to be a world beyond their world, they're willing to check it out anyway.

Now you could argue that they're just trying to appease a whining little sister. But Edmund certainly doesn't seem to care about Lucy's feelings. He could easily stay in the hall and say, "Go to it, kids. I personally don't fall for that kind of rot." So why does he go with her to see what's in the wardrobe? We can assume it's because he's really and truly curious. Lucy is awfully sincere about asking. Something obviously happened to her. So maybe there's something to it after all? And if there *is* . . . well, that would mean life is a bigger adventure than any of them ever suspected!

The fact that Lucy's siblings agree to come and see for themselves indicates that deep down, they're longing for this newfound world to be true. They really want to know if Lucy has found something life-changing. And her invitation is compelling enough that they're willing to give it a try.

The scenario is familiar. Where have we heard it before? Ah, yes: the Gospels. When some guys asked Jesus where he was off to in this great adventure, he said, "Come and see" (see John 1:36-39). Elsewhere, followers of Jesus told a friend that they'd found the King. When that friend responded with skepticism, one of them exclaimed, "Come and see for yourself" (John 1:46). Then there was the woman at the well described in

John 4. After a life-transforming conversation with the
Teacher, she ran and told her village, "Come and see a
man who told me everything I ever did!" And the Bible
tells us that "the people came streaming from the village
to see him" (verses 29-30).

Followers of Jesus recognize that it's not enough
simply to tell others about him. Instead, they're so excited
that they invite others to meet him personally, to experience
for themselves what he's like. "Here's my story," they say.
"Now jump into the story for yourself."

We could argue that Lewis was deliberately echoing the
biblical invitation to "come and see"—particularly since
the phrase shows up earlier in his tiny novella *The Great
Divorce*. After a fantastical bus ride from hell to heaven, a
group of visitors are invited by the inhabitants to check
the place out.[11] The contexts of Lewis's stories and the
Gospel narratives are similar: Some folks have an amazing
adventure that changes their lives, and they want to spread
the word. Not only that but they want their friends to
give it a shot personally, to have the same experience, to
join the adventure. There *is* a Kingdom beyond this world

after all, they exclaim, and wouldn't it be great if we could all be in it together?

Sometimes we, too, are so excited about what God is doing in our lives that we want our friends to get in on the adventure. And that's the interesting part. When we extend the invitation to our friends to come and see what this faith business is all about, they're often willing to give it a try— even the most sneering and cynical and skeptical of the lot. If nothing else, we've piqued their curiosity by our own enthusiasm. We're awfully earnest about it. Obviously something has happened to us. But the real secret is, deep down inside, they yearn for the Kingdom of God to be true. What if the door of faith really does open? What if the Kingdom really does exist? Well, that would mean life is a bigger adventure than they ever expected! Better to take a look than never try.

Now this is where things get difficult. As we learn from Lucy's experience, the invitation does not always lead to an open door—at least, not right away. The whole thing backfires for Lucy the first time, actually. No amount of banging on the back of the wardrobe creates the entrance to another world, and Lucy earns the distrust and ridicule of her siblings. It's a painful experience, and one that takes some time to heal. But the unhappy fact remains: Her attempt to convince them doesn't work.

So what about us? Is the door to faith always open when we invite our friends to check it out? Not always. Perhaps the timing isn't right for them because their hearts aren't soft enough yet. Or maybe God wants them to find their way in by using a different sequence of events than we ourselves experienced. After all, just because a certain spiritual encounter—that life-changing retreat or concert or book—worked for us, that doesn't mean it will work for others.

Unhappily for us, not all our attempts work every time when it comes to helping our friends find the otherworld of God's Kingdom. And this can feel pretty discouraging. It's one of the reasons we tend to give up when our attempts fail at first. Not only do we start questioning the validity of our own spiritual experience, but we feel the great chasm that opens up between people who hold differ-ent belief systems. We're alienated from them in ways we can't explain—and they're often bewildered too: "This faith stuff doesn't work, so why does she insist on believing it? It's so frustrating." Slowly you might even begin to drift apart from each other.

Meanwhile, the Kingdom is calling. There, beyond the door, is a land more amazing than anything in this world. And by golly, no matter what your friends say, you're going to live like it's true. You're going to continue hanging out near the door, trying it now and then, having further adventures of your own.

Even if your friends never believe, don't give up. In the end, you can only tell them your own experience and extend the invitation to them. That's about it. You can't force spiritual adventures on people. You can only ask them to "come and see" for themselves. The rest is up to God.

You can't argue people into the Kingdom of God; you can only share your own experience and invite them to come and see. Have you extended the invitation to your friends lately?

Come and see what our God has done,

    what awesome miracles he performs for people!

Psalm 66:5

Further In

- Who are some of the people who have invited you to experience the Kingdom of God for yourself? How have you responded to their invitation?

- List experiences that have been important in your journey of faith (youth retreats, camps, concerts, books, movies, worship experiences, conversations, even traumas or losses). Why might those experiences work for you but not for someone else?

- How can you share your faith story with friends without getting bogged down in spiritual debates that aren't winnable (e.g., whether or not Adam and Eve had belly buttons!)?

- Why is patience an important part of your relationships with nonbelieving friends?

- What are you going to do about it?

The Word on Inviting Others to "Come and See"

Take some time to read one or more of the following Bible passages:

PSALM 66:16-20; 145:1-7; LUKE 24:9-12; JOHN 4:39-42; 1 PETER 3:13-16

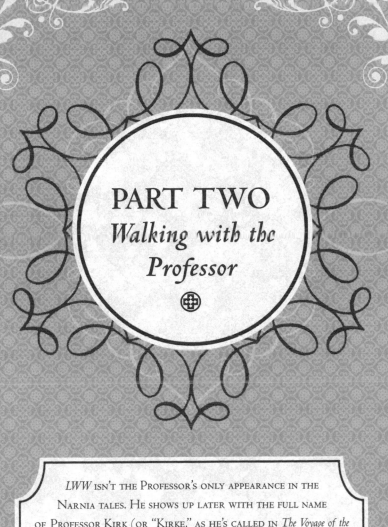

PART TWO
Walking with the Professor

LWW isn't the Professor's only appearance in the Narnia tales. He shows up later with the full name of Professor Kirk (or "Kirke," as he's called in *The Voyage of the "Dawn Treader"*) and still later (or shall we say earlier?) as the boy Digory in *The Magician's Nephew*. And while he doesn't walk with the Pevensies on this particular adventure into the otherworld, he has a good understanding of what they're up against. All they have to do is ask.

The Master Teacher

THERE COMES A POINT in our maturity when we realize that we're really not grown up enough to handle the problems that come our way—at least, not by ourselves and especially not when the health and well-being of a friend or family member is at stake. We can't go it alone. We need someone to guide us, to give us advice. Someone who's been this way before.

Though they don't realize it, the Pevensies are staying with a man who knows a thing or two about other worlds. The Professor, as he's simply called in *The Lion, the Witch and the Wardrobe*, has had some adventures of his own. But to Peter and Susan, who know nothing about him (other than the fact that he seems wise), their host is simply the only adult they can talk to about Lucy's troubling behavior. Their parents are out of the picture, back in London, so the Professor is the substitute. And thank goodness! Here's a mentor worth studying under, for sure.

His character is in some ways an echo of C. S. Lewis himself. The Oxford professor took in children from London during the air raids of World War II, and he had a wardrobe in his house that supposedly intrigued one of them very much.[12] Lewis was also considered an excellent tutor by many of his students, and despite his colleagues' general disapproval of his popular books, his lectures at the university were always packed. As one scholar writes, "He had the master teacher's talent for establishing rapport with his pupils."[13]

But the Professor in *LWW* is also a caricature of some of Lewis's own teachers throughout his life. The teenage Lewis, brilliant though he was, was not above needing such mentors. These were people who challenged and pushed him, broadened his mind, helped him develop "intellectual muscle"—people he turned to for advice and wisdom.

First and most important among those teachers was W. T. Kirkpatrick—simply referred to as "Kirk" in *Surprised by Joy*.[14] Kirkpatrick was a brilliant private tutor who instructed Lewis during several of his high school years. The students affectionately gave this daunting professor the nickname "Great Knock" due to his aggressive way of knocking apart any unthinking, wishy-washy statements they had the foolishness to make. He would yank the rug out from under their best arguments by applying the simple rules of logic and reason (which we'll discuss more in another chapter). From him, Lewis learned the basics of classical debate.

While Kirkpatrick was not a man of faith, Lewis had another mentor who most definitely was. His name was George MacDonald, a Scottish minister and author whom Lewis never met but whose fantasy books had a profound influence on Lewis as a teenager. MacDonald's impact on Lewis was so important, in fact, that Lewis included him as a character in *The Great Divorce*.[15] When the fictional Lewis arrives on the border of heaven, he meets MacDonald, who serves as his guide to what's happening around him. Lewis refers to this kind but stern Scotsman as "my Teacher" throughout the rest of the book.

And now for the really fun trivia! It's quite possible that Professor Kirk not only gets his name from Lewis's own professor Kirkpatrick but from the Scottish word *kirk,* meaning "church." Why? Because Professor Kirk isn't the first person to go by that name in Lewis's fiction. A character called Mother Kirk shows up in *The Pilgrim's Regress,* written long before *The Chronicles of Narnia* came along, and it is she who shows travelers the only way to cross the great canyon of sin.

Are we making any connections yet? Okay, so here's a fun guess: Lewis saw mentors as playing a crucial role in the development of our faith, with the church—or *kirk*—itself being the greatest human teacher we have. And by church we mean not only our local congregation but the scattered believers in every century, around the world, who've embraced the ancient writings of the Christian faith.

So we could argue that the church operates as something of a wise professor in our lives. Not only does it knock apart our feeble arguments against belief but it offers the clearest and best wisdom for reaching the Kingdom of God and for living as Kingdom people in the here and now. And within the church itself are individual "professors"—elders and wise people—whom we can turn to as mentors on our spiritual journeys.

But above all of those is our Master Teacher: Jesus himself.

"Teacher," someone once asked Jesus, "what good deed must I do to have eternal life?" (Matthew 19:16). And another asked, "Teacher, which is the most important commandment in the law of Moses?" (Matthew 22:36). Still another said, "Teacher . . . we know how honest you are. You teach the way of God truthfully" (Matthew 22:16). Clearly Jesus was a wise and learned man—what the Jewish people of his day called a rabbi. Even the other teachers in the community came to him asking questions, including a rather paranoid man by the name of Nicodemus, who only visited at night when he hoped the others weren't watching.

"Rabbi," Nicodemus said in John 3, "we all know that God has sent you to teach us" (John 3:2). "I tell you the truth," Jesus replied, "unless you are born again, you cannot see the Kingdom of God" (verse 3). Poor Nicodemus. He just didn't get the connection. *Born again? How is that possible? And what does that have to do with anything?* They went round and round till Jesus exclaimed, "You are a respected Jewish teacher, and yet you don't understand these things?" (verse 10). We can almost picture Jesus shaking his head, muttering, "Logic! . . . Why don't they teach logic at these schools?"[16] Head knowledge isn't the key to the Kingdom, Jesus was saying. You must let God transform you utterly from the inside out.

The Master Teacher had his own education as a youth. His parents once found him in the Temple in Jerusalem having discussions with the religious scholars of his day (see Luke 2:41-50). Hmm. Why would he be discussing questions if he didn't want to hear the answers? Well, even Jesus was interested in the wisdom of those who had been studying God all their lives. For obvious reasons (um, because he *is* God), he surpasses them all, but this doesn't keep him from wanting to spend time in their presence, soaking up the scholarly atmosphere of the ancient Temple—which, incidentally, is the architectural and spiritual precursor to the church, the *kirk*.

We, too, must seek human mentors for our journey of faith. Sometimes, like the Great Knock, they might not be Christians at all, but something about them challenges and sharpens our own beliefs. Others, like George Mac-Donald and C. S. Lewis himself, may be people we've never met but whose faith-filled writings change our lives. These are the people who show us the way to the Kingdom of God because they've been there before us. It's up to us to ask.

You must seek the wisdom of those who've entered the Kingdom before you. Who's *your* Professor Kirk?

Those who came before us will teach you. They will teach you the wisdom of old.
JOB 8:10

Further In

- Make a list of some of the "professors" who have helped you grow and mature as a person and as a

Christian. Don't limit yourself to people you've actually met; include some of your heroes, such as athletes, politicians, musicians, or authors of any century.

- Who has helped you develop spiritual and intellectual "muscle" rather than flabby, wishy-washy faith?

- What role does the church itself play in helping you develop spiritual and intellectual "muscle"?

- How can you be a mentor to others who are seeking the Kingdom of God?

- What are you going to do about it?

The Word on Seeking Master Teachers

Take some time to read one or more of the following Bible passages:

JOB 12:12-13; PSALM 37:30-31; PROVERBS 4:1-7; 9:9-12; 1 PETER 5:5-6

The Trilemma

IF YOU'VE SPENT ANY TIME in chat rooms, you've probably come across the occasional rant that goes something like this:

> im soooooo sick of this christian garbage no1
> believs that stuff anymore about jesus being god
> or whtever i mean he was nice & reely smart like
> that enlightned buddah dude but not god. he
> was just human a good teacher, ok? when R U
> losers gonna get it?!!!!

Hmm. This person clearly has never read *The Lion, the Witch and the Wardrobe.*

Wait, you say. What exactly does *LWW* have to do with it? Well, if we dig a little deeper into Lewis's other writings, we discover an interesting parallel between the Professor's argument in favor of Lucy's claim to be telling the truth and Lewis's own argument in favor of Jesus' claim to be God. It's called the *trilemma,*[17] or a choice with only three options, only one of which is the logical solution.

Let's start with the Professor's arguments.

Lucy claims to have passed through the wardrobe into a magical land called Narnia. Her siblings simply can't get past that point. They try to humor her, cajole her, and argue with her, but it's no good. And even though Edmund knows she's telling the truth, he joins the side of Peter and Susan. But it doesn't matter. Lucy won't budge from what she believes to be the facts. It's her story, and she's stickin' to it.

When Peter and Susan approach the Professor about their sister's behavior, asking his advice on what to do, they're astonished at his ready acceptance of what Lucy has to say for herself. As the Professor suggests, "There are only three possibilities." She's a pathological liar, or she's clinically insane, or she's speaking the truth. Clearly she's not crazy, he says, because you can tell just by looking at her. And since she isn't one to tell lies, then the only remaining option is that she's being utterly honest.

It's a similar argument to one Lewis makes about Jesus. Lewis tackles this topic in several different places, most famously in book 2, chapter 3 of *Mere Christianity*, as well as in the lesser-known essay "What Are We to Make of Jesus Christ?" in *God in the Dock*. Both of these are must-reads for anyone who takes the Christian faith seriously. But in the meantime, here's a look at the trilemma we face.

To begin with, Jesus never budged from his claim to be God. No matter what people may say to the contrary, you simply can't get around statements like "If you trust me, you are trusting not only me, but also God who sent me. For when you see me, you are seeing the one who sent me" (John 12:44-45). So, Lewis argues, we're to accept none of this nonsense about Jesus being just "a great moral teacher."[18] Good teachers don't make absurd claims and then expect you to accept everything else they say too.

No, Jesus was one of only three things: (1) clinically insane; (2) an egotistical, pathological liar; *or* (3) exactly who he said he was: the Son of God. A breakdown of each of these possibilities yields some interesting insights.

Option #1: Was Jesus crazy? If we give close scrutiny to the stories about Jesus we find in the Gospel narratives, we can learn a lot by the way people reacted to him. As Lewis says, people either feared him or loved him, but nobody treated him with mere "mild approval."[19] People were astonished at the way he taught: He had more knowledge and authority than some of their religious leaders (see Luke 4:31-32). Clearly, this was no raving lunatic.

And take, for example, Jesus' encounter with the demon-possessed man in Mark 5:1-19. The contrast between the two men is startling. Jesus speaks with power and authority; the madman screamed and begged and groveled. However, once the demoniac was set free from the evil hold on him, he was "clothed and perfectly sane" (verse 15). Jesus had a calming influence on him rather than the reverse.

Wait a minute: Generally speaking, being around other crazy people makes us feel like we, too, are losing our minds. This is not a story about two guys who both need to be institutionalized. It's about a sane man who restores a crazy man to his right mind.

Another point is that if Jesus had been truly off his rocker, people wouldn't have taken him so seriously. They would have laughed at him at best or tried to lock him up in a mental institution at worst. We never see any of them simply shaking their heads in pity, the way we do when the harmless "village idiot" stumbles by, muttering under his breath. No, like Lucy in *LWW,* apparently all it took was one look at Jesus to tell that he was perfectly sane in every respect.

Now, let's tackle option #2: Was Jesus a pathological liar? Well, if he was lying about being the Son of God, then we can't trust anything else he said either.

Which means that all the beautiful teachings in the Gospels that even non-Christians respect—such as the Sermon on the Mount (Matthew 5–7), the Golden Rule (Luke 6:31), and the Beatitudes (Matthew 5:3-10)—must be tossed into the garbage. What about "Do not judge others, and you will not be judged" (Luke 6:37)? Chuck it. "Love each other" (John 15:17)? Chuck that too. "Give, and you will receive" (Luke 6:38)? Can't have that either. And while we're at it, might as well throw out the Lord's Prayer (Matthew 6:9-13) and the most famous verse of all time, John 3:16: "For God loved the world so much that he gave his one and only Son, so that everyone who believes in him will not perish but have eternal life." Guess that means no more giant banners in the stands at NFL games.

In short, you can't have the truths without the Truth. Either Jesus is telling the truth about himself, or he is lying about everything else too. None of this business about Jesus being merely an enlightened Buddha of sorts, offering wiser-than-average insights into how to live a healthy, balanced life. None of this quoting of Jesus in order to make your own point about justice or fairness or peace on earth when you don't really believe what Jesus said about himself. Like Lucy, if Jesus can be trusted on all other points, then he can be trusted on this point too.

Which brings us to option #3: He was telling the truth. Since, with the Professor's help, we've ruled out the first two options, we're left with the conclusion that Jesus was in fact the Son of God, just as he said. Of course, Jesus himself was continually asserting his trustworthiness on this and all points, often prefacing one of his statements or stories with "I tell you the truth" or "truly." In fact, he not only says he's the way to God but he says he *is* the Truth (see John 14:6). The reason he teaches such compelling stuff about the Kingdom of God is because he is the King. And who knows better about the Kingdom than the King himself?

If we're going to walk very far with the Professor, we'll have to make a decision on this trilemma eventually. As Lewis so astutely put it, "Christians believe that Jesus Christ is the Son of God because He said so. The other evidence about Him has convinced them that He was neither a lunatic nor a quack."[20] Which will you choose?

Jesus can only be one of three things: a liar, a crazy person, or the King he claims to be. Will you take his word for it?

You will know the truth, and the truth will set you free.
John 8:32

Further In

- What's wrong with believing that Jesus was nothing more than just a good moral teacher?

- How tempting is it for you to ignore or dismiss Jesus' claim to be God?

- What are your favorite sayings of Jesus from the Gospels (Matthew, Mark, Luke, and John), and which ones are the most difficult for you to accept?

- What arguments will you offer the next time someone insists that Jesus was just another "enlightened" man, like Buddha or Gandhi? How will you defend your faith in Christ?

- What are you going to do about it?

Taking Jesus at His Word

Take some time to read one or more of the following Bible passages:

MATTHEW 3:16-17; MARK 14:60-62; LUKE 22:67-71;
JOHN 7:40-41; 8:13-18, 48-49

PART THREE
Walking with Susan

She's not prone to believing in other worlds,
and she sure doesn't feel safe once she gets there.
But Susan has a knack for asking the honest, practical
questions we all long to know in this Kingdom
quest. The trouble is: Are the answers
what we want to hear?

Uncommon Sense

As EDMUND POINTS OUT from the very beginning (and it
would take an annoying little brother to bring this up!),
Susan is trying to fill a parental role in the absence of
their mother and father. Who is *she* to tell them it's time
for bed? Then once they get to Narnia, she's the one who
suggests they take the coats with them to stay warm. She's
also the one to worry about such concerns as what they'll
find to eat along the way.

In short, walking with Susan means we'll be taking the
most practical, sensible route.

And that's okay, up to a point. Her common sense is often helpful, and the others are glad to have her along. But even before the children enter Narnia, we see some cracks developing in Susan's sensible exterior, particularly when it comes to approaching the Professor about what to do with Lucy.

Susan uses what she probably feels are very grown-up arguments against believing Lucy's story. The possibility of there being another world just doesn't seem plausible. But before we get even four lines into the discussion, we realize that Susan's common sense is no match for the Professor's logic.

The basic principles of logic dictate that a statement cannot be both true and false at the same time (the law of contradiction) and that a statement *must* be either true or false (the law of the excluded middle).[21] We see these laws at work in the trilemma posed by the Professor. Lucy is lying, or she is crazy, or she is telling the truth. She can't be some combination, and she can't be *none* of those things (whoa . . .). The laws of logic dictate that she must be one of them. Which is the most likely?

Notice how practical common sense about the supposed impossibility of other worlds doesn't come into the equation.

As Susan discovers, some truths are not necessarily the most obvious or sensible at first glance. They often require *uncommon* sense. To give an everyday example: You would think that the chances of finding two people at a party who share the same birthday would be pretty slim. After all, there are 365 days in a year. But oddly enough, the rules of statistics tell us that the chances are better than 50 percent in a group of more than twenty-three people.[22] Just because something isn't obvious doesn't make it nonsensical. There's a pattern, a rhyme, a reason to it.

And the same is true with the Christian faith. Even though at some point we must admit that logic only goes so far in explaining everything about what we believe, we certainly have a very plausible case for believing what we do. Not only do we have the authority of God's Word to rely on but we follow in the footsteps of many intelligent people who've accepted Christianity on the basis of some very powerful arguments in its favor.

Blaise Pascal was a seventeenth-century French mathematician and philosopher perhaps best known for the triangle that bears his name. But he was also a Christian, albeit a struggling one (aren't we all!). His gambler's interest in the mathematical principles of statistics and probability led him to pose a wager to his atheist friends that can be (very) roughly summarized like this: "Fine. Let's say that you're right and I'm wrong about the existence of God. Well then, in the end, we all lose. Death is the winner. But let's say that I'm right and you're wrong. Well, then you've *still* lost, while I've won infinite happiness in heaven for eternity."

He was no fool. If there's only one option that leads to a winning outcome, why bet on anything else?

C. S. Lewis followed squarely in this intellectual tradition in his defense of the Christian faith. As we've already discussed, the climate of Oxford academia seemed incompatible with his forays into Christian apologetics. But even in this community that saw Christianity as intellectually foggy, Lewis was able to make faith not only plausible but highly probable. "At the end of the day you may not agree with him," says one scholar, "but Christianity is no longer this sort of mindless beliefism. He believed that there's a reason for accepting these things and you can't just write it off."[23]

Lewis's argument in favor of Jesus' claim to be God (as we discussed in the previous chapter) is perhaps the most famous example. Note how he argued his position from the standpoint of logic rather than from practicality or common sense. Common sense would tell you that a regular, Joe Schmo human being can't also be a holy, perfect God. But uncommon sense tells a completely different story, and one that can't be quickly or easily discounted.

Nicodemus faced just such a conundrum in his midnight visit to Jesus (see John 3). We've already mentioned his struggle to grasp what Jesus meant by the statement "Unless you are born again, you cannot see the Kingdom of God" (verse 3). Nicodemus scratched his head: "How can an old man go back into his mother's womb and be born again?" he asked (verse 4). But Jesus wasn't talking about *physical* rebirth; he was talking about *spiritual* rebirth. Think like a logician: *If* our sinful nature is what keeps us out of the

Kingdom, *then* we must get rid of that sinful nature in order to enter it. And *if* our sinful nature is something we're born with, *then* only death of some kind will free us from it. Therefore, *if* we're going to participate in the Kingdom, *then* we must experience the death of our old sinful nature and be given a new nature. We must start over somehow. To use a famous metaphor, we must be born again.

Head hurt yet? Feel like you're going over the edge? So does Susan when she hears the Professor's uncommon sense. When she realizes their host is being perfectly serious, her final, most desperate question boils down to practicalities: "But what are we to do?"

Sometimes it feels like you're being asked, like Susan, to put aside your common sense and get a little crazy when it comes to this Kingdom quest. And yet making the leap isn't necessarily making a leap into the dark, though it may feel like it. It's making a leap into the light. Things that didn't make sense before actually seem clearer, more logical, once you give it a shot. You're not dismissing common sense; you're recognizing that it doesn't necessarily take you far enough.

C. S. Lewis, perhaps better than anybody in the past one hundred years, argued that we don't check our brains at the door when we become Christians. Sure, the Christian faith may seem to have a lot of holes in it sometimes. You won't be able to argue every point and win (and you certainly can't argue someone into the Kingdom, as we discussed before). But your faith *is* defensible, as defensible as any other worldview out there, and far more plausible and even probable than many.

> **Believing in God's Kingdom is not always "sensible" or practical, but it *is* plausible. Will you make the leap into the Light?**
>
> *Don't let anyone capture you with empty philosophies and high-sounding nonsense that come from human thinking and from the spiritual powers of this world, rather than from Christ.*
> Colossians 2:8

Further In

• When is it helpful to have common sense—a practical response to solving a problem?

- In what ways does the Christian faith seem implausible or simply unbelievable to you? How will you live according to the uncommon sense of the Gospel stories?

- People often argue that faith just isn't practical (e.g., "I just don't have time for church" or "I don't have enough money to give to the soup kitchen"). What's really at the heart of their objections?

- How can you show that faith in the God of the Bible is both reasonable and plausible?

- What are you going to do about it?

The Word on Uncommon Sense

Take some time to read one or more of the following Bible passages:

PROVERBS 3:5-6; 1 CORINTHIANS 1:18-27; 4:1-4; 1 TIMOTHY 6:20-21; 2 TIMOTHY 2:23-26

Safety First?

WE ALL HAVE FRIENDS LIKE THIS: the ones who won't touch the locker room door handle with their bare hands or sip from our straws. "But I don't have a cold!" you protest, even as your clean-freak friend jumps up to get a drink of her own. Her backpack is full of hand sanitizers and wipes and antiseptic spray. "Don't touch that," she warns about the daddy longlegs making its way across the biology lab windowsill. You roll your eyes. Is *anything* safe?

Enter Susan Pevensie. She's usually the first among her siblings to express any kind of fear or hesitation in this

Narnia adventure, and it's more than just her need to act according to practical common sense. This caution is born out of her desire to avoid getting hurt. "Is he— quite safe?"[24] she asks, upon learning that Aslan is a lion. For Susan—as with many of us, if we're really honest— "Safety first" is the motto.

Our human nature is prone to such fear and distrust. We start out feeling secure in the arms of our parents or guardians, and then one day (perhaps the first day of kindergarten?) we look out at the world and realize things are not as safe as we supposed. There are bullies on the playground. Our bikes crash. We're even taught not to speak to strangers. Life is not safe, so we learn to be cautious when walking out the front door. And—for those of us whose homes *are* the troubled places where pain and trauma happen—we learn to be cautious walking *in* the front door too.

And we treat faith the same way. We want God to be "safe." We want him to place us where there will be no risks, where our comfort and security are givens, where there are guarantees about surviving our experiences unscathed. We want to be able to give to those in need without having to wait on buying that MP3 player for ourselves (to give an example). We want to have all the adventures of a mission trip in a third world country without the possibility of getting lost, injured, or assaulted. We don't want this faith stuff to hurt.

But God makes no such promises. He *does* promise that he is good (see Psalm 136) and that he has our best interests in mind (see Jeremiah 29:11). But he never said anything about being safe.

C. S. Lewis himself admitted, "I am a safety-first creature. Of all arguments against love none makes so strong an appeal to my nature as 'Careful! This might lead you to suffering.'"[25] When it comes to loving God and doing what he says, our fears of feeling pain and losing control often keep us from committing entirely to him. We especially don't want God to start digging around in our business in case he finds something unholy that he needs to remove. We kind of like our unholy things, our private sins and fears. Getting rid of them would be painful. So rather than step into the sacred adventure God has for us, we retreat.

There's a story told in Matthew 14:22-33 about a time the disciples were out on a boat in a storm, on the brink of sinking. Suddenly, they saw Jesus walking toward them over the waves, in the midst of the wind, rising up and down with each crest. The disciple Peter, ever the bold and brash one, called out and asked to be able to walk out to him. And Jesus said to come. So Peter gave it a try. But then he focused on the wind and the waves and lost his nerve. This whole walking-on-water stuff suddenly didn't look so safe after all. And sure enough, he started to sink—pretty quickly, we can imagine. But Jesus reached out his hand.

Jesus never promises that following in his footsteps will be safe, that we will never come to any harm if we obey God the way he did. Jesus' own footsteps led him to suffering and even death. In fact (and we don't really like to think about this), he *promises* that suffering will be part of our journey: "Here on earth you will have many trials and sorrows" (John 16:33). But then he adds, "But take heart, because I have overcome the world." As Mr. Beaver says about Aslan, "'Course he isn't safe. But he's good."[26]

People who've gone through a difficult loss or trauma often say that their faith is shaken. This may be true of you at some point or another. You lose a loved one or are the victim of violence, and you feel knocked out of the safety of God's protective arms. You question his goodness. The spiritual foundation that you thought was so solid seems more like thin ice. But as Jesus said, "Take heart." Just because *your* faith is shaken doesn't mean *the* faith is shaken. The eternal truths of the Kingdom aren't altered or affected by the experience that shook your beliefs.

That's because God's holy character is fixed, immovable. As it says in Hebrews 13:8, "Jesus Christ is the same yesterday, today, and forever." What you're experiencing is what happens to a sapling when it's blown in a mighty wind. Your faith is shaken because your branches are tossed in some storm of life, not because your roots are torn and pulled up by an earthquake. If you stay put, if you cling with all your might to the good foundation of God's holy character, the storm will pass.

Susan eventually becomes Queen Susan the Gentle, no longer concerned for her own safety but full of compassion for the well-being of others. As a grown woman, chasing down the White Stag in the woods with her brothers and sister, she does express caution when one of them makes the suggestion that they follow wherever this lamp-post leads. But after some discussion, she agrees to go wherever the adventure takes them.

What a contrast between this Susan and the one we see at the beginning of the story! She's now willing to take the next step in faith rather than fear. Not only has she learned to trust her siblings but she puts her trust in Aslan, the one who has led them on all their adventures so far. She's willing to go beyond the comfortable world she knows because she has faith in her king.

We must take each step in this Kingdom with faith, not fear. Do you trust your King?

God has not given us a spirit of fear and timidity, but of power, love, and self-discipline.

2 TIMOTHY 1:7

Further In

- When is "safety first" an appropriate attitude toward the dangers of life?

- Why is it not always the appropriate attitude toward following Jesus?

- What are the "unsafe" things Jesus sometimes asks us to do? Why does he ask us to do them?

- How will you trust in God's unshakable character when things aren't going so well?

- What are you going to do about it?

The Word on Safety

Take some time to read one or more of the following Bible passages:

PROVERBS 3:21-26; LUKE 12:6-7; 12:32; 2 CORINTHIANS 1:6-7; HEBREWS 10:35-36; 1 JOHN 4:16-18

PART FOUR
Walking with Edmund

Even before he steps through the wardrobe, the youngest brother is itching to be king of his own life, free from everyone else. He's not about to submit to the authority of his older siblings, much less to the mysteriously absent lord of Narnia. But soon he finds himself a prisoner of his own rebellion. What happens when the price of freedom is higher than we can possibly pay?

Seeing Is Not Believing

LET'S SAY YOUR SMALL WATERCRAFT has just sunk and you're in need of rescue. Desperately. Floating into your vision comes a lifeboat. The problem is, not only is the boat captained by your annoying older brother but you know that once you're brought on board, you'll have to help row at some point. So you refuse to acknowledge that the lifeboat is even there. You won't swim toward it or let anyone from the lifeboat help you out of the water. Instead, you start swimming away as fast as your failing arms will take you.

Basically, being able to see the boat means virtually nothing if you don't act upon what you see. You're going down, whether the lifeboat is there or not.

That's exactly the choice Edmund makes as his Narnia adventure gets underway. He steps through the wardrobe on the heels of Lucy but refuses to acknowledge to Peter and Susan that he has actually seen the magical world with his own eyes. He's not willing to admit that he was wrong. And then later, after they've all gotten in together, he doesn't even apologize. Instead, he distances himself even more from all that is good and noble in Narnia, eventually making the break from his siblings altogether.

Edmund refuses to submit to the truth of what he sees. He uses one excuse after another to justify why he's betraying his family to the Witch. But even as Edmund makes these excuses, it's clear he knows the facts about the Witch's character. He has witnessed her wickedness and cruelty for himself, but he won't admit it. He refuses to believe.

A spiritual principle is at work in this kind of attitude. Otherwise, Jesus wouldn't have had to say, over and over again in the midst of his teachings, "He who has ears to hear, let him hear" (Mark 4:9, NIV). It's an odd statement at first. If you're not deaf, then of *course* you're able to hear what's being said. And yet we know exactly what he's talking about. We've all experienced times when our words to friends go in one ear and out the other or when they insist you said something you honestly never said. They had ears, but they didn't truly listen. Hearing something is not the same as accepting it as truth.

The Old Testament prophets dealt with this same problem when they were trying to get across what God was saying to his stubborn, rebellious people. The prophet Isaiah quoted God, saying that the people "listen carefully, but do not understand" and "watch closely, but learn nothing" (Isaiah 6:9). Centuries later, the early Christians, too, were met with resistance to their message wherever they went (see Acts 7:51-60). Frustrated, they often quoted those Old Testament prophets as proof that, if a person's heart is already closed to spiritual things, then it doesn't matter what kinds of miracles that person sees or what truths that person hears. He or she will refuse to submit.

The people of Jesus' own day were the same way, especially the religious leaders. Despite seeing Jesus perform amazing miracles and hearing the truths of the Kingdom from his own lips, they rejected it all. In fact, several of them even grasped the truth but didn't dare acknowledge it (see John 12:42). They were determined to stay spiritually blind and deaf.

So hearing or even seeing something isn't the same as acknowledging that it's true for your own life. There's a difference between seeing and believing. There are also different *kinds* of seeing for different levels of belief.

Take, for example, the disciple Thomas, affectionately known as the Doubter. According to John 20:24-29, he wanted to see the resurrected Christ for himself before he would be willing to accept what the other disciples claimed to have seen. He wanted proof. He wanted to scientifically verify that the Resurrection actually happened, using his five senses. For him, seeing was believing.

But for others, seeing isn't even close to believing. Lewis wrote about this in an essay entitled "Miracles," in which he described meeting a woman who claimed to have seen a ghost. Apparently, she believed she'd been hallucinating. Without getting into whether or not ghosts could possibly exist, Lewis uses the example to make an important point: We won't accept supernatural events "as miraculous if we already hold a philosophy which excludes the supernatural."[27]

In other words, whatever we have seen can be explained away if we don't choose to believe it. That's why, when someone recovers from an illness after a bunch of people have been praying, other people will say things like, "It wasn't really a miracle; it was just that the cells in her body started to fight the disease." So why, you might ask, did the cells start fighting when they hadn't been before? But of course the person's presupposition is that supernatural miracles don't happen, so your question isn't really "heard."

And then there are people like Edmund. They don't even fall into the category of those who refuse to believe what they see. They fall into the category of those who aren't willing to admit they know the truth, deep down. Pride keeps them from acknowledging openly what they don't want to believe is actually real. Why? Because if it turns out to be true, an uncomfortable spiritual reality will have a claim on their lives. It will mean they're no longer masters of their own destinies. It means there's something or Someone out there who is more in charge than they are.

Some of us—or our friends—may fall into the category of seers but not believers. "Do you believe in Jesus?" you ask, and they say, "Yes!" Careful now. Don't let it drop there. Ask, "What do you mean by belief in Jesus?" Because simply believing in the existence of Jesus as a historical figure isn't enough. As one youth worker has said, "Believing in God is not the issue; believing God *matters* is the issue."[28] We must believe that Jesus' life, death, and resurrection actually have a divine purpose.

Right. But believing he died for our sins isn't enough either, though it may sound scandalous to say so. Think about it: Sometimes when you probe, you find out your friend merely believes that there once was a historical figure named Jesus who only *thought* he was dying to save us from our sins. Whether your friend thinks Jesus' death actually accomplished our salvation is a different matter. Yikes!

Okay, so probe a little further. Does your friend believe Jesus is the Son of God, the King of the universe? Yes? All well and good. So do the demons, though they refuse to submit to his authority (see James 2:19). Yikes again! No, to be painfully blunt, none of our friends' statements of belief really matter unless they can say, in so many words, "Yes, and Jesus is *my* King too. I've surrendered my life to him. I'm on his side and want to do his will." Until they can say this, there's reason to question if they've really accepted the truth.

Walking with Edmund forces us to consider how honest we are about what our spiritual eyes have seen and our spiritual ears have heard. Have you asked yourself the tough questions lately?

It's not enough to merely acknowledge that the King exists. How will you act on the truth of what you've seen?

We live by believing and not by seeing.
2 CORINTHIANS 5:7

Further In

• Why do some people say they need proof of God's existence before they'll believe in him?

• How easy or difficult is it to explain away things like miracles? Why isn't scientific proof enough to guarantee faith?

• What does it mean to be spiritually blind or deaf?

• How tempting is it for you to ignore the truths you see in the Bible and not act on them?

• What are you going to do about it?

The Word on Spiritual Sight

Take some time to read one or more of the following Bible passages:

DEUTERONOMY 29:2-9; MATTHEW 13:10-17; JOHN 9:35-41; 12:35-43; ACTS 28:23-28; 2 PETER 1:16-19; 1 JOHN 1:1-3

The Breaking Point

DID C. S. LEWIS nail family dynamics, or what? Edmund is constantly angry at Peter for being in charge and feels like second or even third best most of the time. You can imagine them bickering in the train on the way to the Professor's house: "You took my seat!" "Oh, don't be a little pig." "But that's where I wanted to sit!" "And what makes you so important?" "Yeah? Well, who made you king, anyway?" "Oh, bother. Just take it. I don't care."

Sarah Arthur

Edmund is always thinking of himself and what he deserves. It's all about his rights. And unfortunately, we can relate.

How many of us have been in similar fights with our siblings or parents over who got the most Christmas presents or over how unfair it is that so-and-so gets the car when it's our turn? We've all protested about getting a low grade when that other guy didn't even study and can't even write a complete sentence. And how come Britney or Kelsey or whatever-her-name-is always gets first chair or first string, while you sit down the line, warming the bench?

And while we're at it, isn't it about time someone else signed up for the soup kitchen for a change? You haven't had a free Saturday morning in weeks. And seriously: If your older brother bosses you around one more time, you're about ready to blow your stack. It's just not fair. You've got your rights, same as everyone else; you deserve better.

Oh really? Let's consider one example given by C. S. Lewis.

As the busload of "ghosts" in Lewis's *The Great Divorce* arrive in heaven, one of them encounters a bright "spirit" who was once one of his employees—and a convicted murderer, no less. The ghost is incredulous. He can't believe this guy ended up in heaven while he's been in hell all this time. Even as the spirit tries to convince the ghost that none of that matters anymore, the ghost exclaims, "I'm asking for nothing but my rights." The heavenly being explains, "I haven't got my rights, or I should not be here."[29]

In other words, if we insist on having what we "deserve," then hell will be our dwelling place forever. Because that's what we all deserve. Our sins have earned us a spot there. But if we, like the bright spirit, are willing to surrender our stubborn, rebellious wills to God, we'll be offered grace and forgiveness that we don't deserve.

As one writer put it, "It is not a question of giving up sin, but of giving up my right to myself, my natural independence and self-assertiveness, and this is where the battle has to be fought." Then he added, "Beware of refusing to go to the funeral of your own independence."[30]

Ouch. It doesn't sound like this discussion of personal rights is headed in an advantageous direction. We're not sure we like hearing that at some point in this adventure of faith, our stubborn wills have to be broken, that we must reach the breaking point. We must surrender. We're not merely sorry sinners in need of a little assistance; we are, as Lewis says in *Mere Christianity*, rebels who must lay down our arms.

At one point in his gradual conversion process, Lewis felt as if he were being offered a choice. He could hang on to everything for himself, or he could let it go. When he finally gave in, it was as "the most dejected and reluctant convert in all England."[31] First he turned to theism (belief in a God), and then it was a short walk to Christianity. But the breaking point came before everything else.

One of the most famous parables of Jesus is known as the story of the lost son (see Luke 15:11-32). This kid decides he has had enough of living under the rule of his dad and older brother, so he takes his share of the inheritance and runs away to party. It isn't until he's broke and desperate that he realizes just how stupid he has been. He has to reach the breaking point before he'll give up. (Incidentally, isn't it interesting that this is the *younger* son? Sounds somewhat familiar. . . .)

As we go through the Bible, we encounter stubborn people who must give in and surrender to God. In the Old Testament, the beloved and popular King David had to face his selfish wrongdoing in sleeping with another man's wife and having that man killed (see 2 Samuel 12:1-14). Then there's Jesus' disciple Peter, who lied about their friendship once Jesus was arrested (see Mark 14:66-72). It isn't until after Jesus' predictions about Peter's denial come true that Peter broke down and sobbed. And we can't forget the religious headhunter Paul, who was struck temporarily blind before he finally surrendered his life to Christ (see Acts 9:1-9).

For all of us—Edmund included—reaching the breaking point has to do with giving up our right to do what we please and choosing instead to do only the will of the King. That's the moment when everything changes. It's no longer about me, me, me. We don't care about our own personal rights anymore.

Edmund's breaking point comes after he has been taken prisoner by the White Witch and suffers at her hands. Then, for the first time, he actually has one thought about someone other than himself. He speaks out on behalf of the little Christmas party in the woods, moments before the Witch turns them to stone. And as a result, he suffers even more. But soon he stops caring altogether. Once his will is broken, he no longer thinks about himself. It's our first glimpse that there might be some hope for Edmund after all.

And that's the wonderful thing. When we reach the breaking point—when we let go of our own rights, when we surrender our will to God—he employs us in advocating for the rights of others. "Speak up for those who cannot speak for themselves," we're told (Proverbs 31:8). "Seek justice. Help the oppressed. Defend the cause of orphans. Fight for the rights of widows" (Isaiah 1:17). Instead of spending all our time arguing for what we think we deserve, we now speak up for the single mom who needs help paying for day care, for instance, or on behalf of the inner-city neighborhood that hasn't had garbage pickup in months.

By the end of the book, Edmund is no longer standing before his imaginary judge, arguing for the right to do just as he pleases: to be prince of Narnia and eat all the Turkish delight he wants. He has "got past thinking about himself."[32] Instead, he becomes King Edmund the Just, defending the rights of others.

We must reach the breaking point before we'll surrender to the will of the King. What's the breaking point for you?

If any of you wants to be my follower, you must turn from your selfish ways.
Mark 8:34

Further In

• What do you do when you feel like things are unfair?

• Why isn't God impressed when you complain about your own rights and your own way?

• What keeps you from surrendering to his will?

• What are some ways you can stop putting yourself first and instead take a stand for the rights of others?

• What are you going to do about it?

The Word on Surrender
Take some time to read one or more of the following Bible passages:

PSALM 51:1-12; MARK 8:34-38; JOHN 12:24-25; 1 JOHN 3:16

PART FIVE
Walking with Peter

As the eldest brother and the future High King of Narnia, Peter has the weight of responsibility on his shoulders. This newfound world is not without its dangers and desires. If we're going to walk in the footsteps of Peter, we'd better ready ourselves for battle. But along the way, we just might earn a crown.

Heart's Desire

IT'S A BIT LIKE being in love for the first time.

You hear his or her voice on the other end of the phone, and your heart does a little flip. Part of it is happiness at being on this person's radar. Part of it is your intense longing to be on his or her radar forever. And part of it is fear mixed with a strange sort of grief that what if for some reason this is the last time you ever hear from this person. Joy, longing, fear—they wash over you in an instant and then disappear.

When the Beavers inform the children that Aslan is on the move, the children feel a strange stirring in their hearts. Peter in particular makes what seems like a casual statement: He says he's "longing" to meet this Aslan. We might be inclined to overlook the sentence altogether, thinking perhaps he means that he's merely interested or curious, as anyone would be when told that the king of a magical land happens to be a lion. But he doesn't say he's curious; he says he's longing, and that carries a very different meaning, when you give it some thought.

To long for something means you've had it in your mind for a while, the way you fix your heart on getting that iPod for Christmas or save up for months to buy that used Honda. Or, more important, the way you dream about that perfect spouse or ideal career. *Longing* carries with it the concept of *desire*; your heart and soul are bound up in wanting this thing, as if the desire comes out of nowhere, beyond yourself, and will not be satisfied until you have whatever it is. It implies a sense of time; it implies that you've been waiting.

So how can Peter have been waiting for Aslan? He hadn't even heard of the king of Narnia till just that day, when Mr. Beaver first mentioned him in the wood. If Peter didn't know about Aslan, how could he have been longing for him? After applying the Professor's brand of logic to such a question, we might conclude that Peter's desire to meet Aslan began before he ever knew who Aslan was. He yearned for something nameless, still undefined in his mind.

Yearning. Desire. It's a theme that weaves throughout the life and works of C. S. Lewis. In *Surprised by Joy,* he introduced the concept of longing as the signature quest of his childhood and young adulthood. Every once in a while— when interacting with a particularly beautiful story or work of art—he would experience what he could only describe as the unbidden, fleeting desire for something he couldn't yet name. The best he could come up with was *joy,* an elusive, poignant, almost painful kind of elation that left as quickly as it came. There's no trying to make it last, no trying to repeat it. The feeling arrived unbidden from somewhere outside the self and went back to whatever world it came from.

Have you ever felt that sudden stab of longing? The desire for something that has no name but washes over you unexpectedly and leaves just as quickly as it comes? Perhaps it's while you're listening to a particularly poignant strain of music. Or maybe it's when you're just coming around the bend of some trail high in the Sierra Nevadas. Some people have experienced it in the movie theater while watching scenes from *The Lord of the Rings* or while reading chapters of a science fiction novel in the dark of night, alone in the quiet of an otherwise empty house.

Why this ache when we experience something so beautiful or strange? Where does this longing come from? And what are we longing for? Why can't we define it, exactly? For Lewis, as he gradually came to accept the claims of Jesus, the answer grew more and more clear: "If I find in myself a desire which no experience in this world can satisfy, the most probable explanation is that I was made for another world."[33]

As we said in the opening section of this book, we're all longing for the Kingdom of God. And at the heart of that yearning is the desire to know and be known by the King himself.

Until Jesus came along, all that God's people had were prophecies about the coming of the King mixed with stabs of desire: the desperate quest to know God personally, the poignant yearning to walk with him and talk with him. And yet when they finally did see him, real and alive and in the flesh, they were confronted with their own doubts about who he really was. Only a few, like Peter in *LWW*, acknowledged their King immediately.

Take Simeon and Anna, for example. It was barely a week after Jesus' birth when his parents brought him to the Temple to be circumcised (see Luke 2:25-38). There an old man named Simeon—who was "eagerly waiting for the Messiah to come and rescue Israel" (verse 25)—suddenly recognized the baby as the One he had been waiting for. He gathered Jesus in his arms and began praising God. Meanwhile, an elderly widow named Anna, who had spent most of her life praying in the Temple, also drew near and began doing the same thing. Needless to say, Jesus' parents were amazed and probably a bit alarmed.

The point is that these two aged, humble prophets recognized their King when they saw him. Even though there was no crown on his little newborn head and no trumpet announcing the arrival of God's own Prince, they could finally put a name to what they'd been yearning for all those years. And after this incident, Anna in particular "talked about [Jesus] to everyone who had been waiting expectantly for God to rescue Jerusalem" (verse 38). God was "on the move," and Anna didn't want anyone to miss out.

It wasn't until Lewis converted to Christianity that he eventually realized what he'd been longing for: God. Not the Norse gods of the pagan world, not even the gods or spirits of fantasy worlds, but the God of the Bible—a real, living Being in whom we can have life forever. The same can be true for each of us. When we recognize the Creator and Lord of the universe, we have a name for what we've been waiting and hoping for. His name is Jesus, and he's the King.

Some of us have friends who've experienced that sense of yearning but have no name for it yet. They feel their soul pierced by something like hope or joy, or they glimpse for a brief moment a higher, holier kind of life and yearn to be a part of it, but they don't know where it comes from. Many of them try to feed or quench that desire by pursuing whatever they think might work: romance, mysticism, good deeds (done in the name of duty or humanism), even extreme sports. Others try to dull the ache through chemical highs, sexual thrills, or petty crime.

Since we are their friends, part of our role is to help them understand that their longing comes from an inborn desire to know the King of the universe. And, like the Beavers with Peter, we are to tell our friends about the King—that his return is imminent, that he is on the move even now.

We're all longing to meet the true King. Will you recognize his name when you hear it? Will you help others to do the same?

I am worn out waiting for your rescue,
> *but I have put my hope in your word.*

My eyes are straining to see your promises come true.
PSALM 119:81-82

Further In

• What are you truly longing for, if you can
  name it?

• What events or experiences trigger that longing in
  you (e.g., a certain strain of music, a scent, a
  photo)?

• What are some ways your non-Christian friends
  try to quench their elusive sense of longing or
  desire, apart from God?

• Why don't any of those "solutions," other than
  God himself, work?

• What are you going to do about it?

The Word on Longing

Take some time to read one or more of the following Bible passages:

PSALM 73:25-26; 84:1-3; JEREMIAH 32:40; LUKE 1:67-70;
ROMANS 8:23-25

The Weight of Kingship

YOUR PARENTS ARE GONE for the weekend, and to your complete embarrassment, they've asked a friend to stay with you and your siblings, even though you're all practically old enough to vote. Do your parents think that you'll throw some wild party or something? that you'll trash the house? No, nothing so tame. They think you're going to kill each other.

Yep, sibling rivalry is alive and well. As the guys wrestle in the kitchen to prove who's the alpha male, the girls hiss at one other in the bathroom, and everyone battles for a higher place in the pecking order. And just because you might be older doesn't necessarily mean much.

But it means something to the Pevensies. For Peter in particular, being the eldest is a role he takes seriously. With the parents out of the picture, Peter's in charge, an arrangement that doesn't suit Edmund one bit. Who is *Peter* to tell him what to do? Edmund is *just as important*, by gum, and he's going to prove it. By contrast, Peter's perspective on being the leader is not about getting the props he thinks he deserves but about taking care of the others.

It's an important principle for C. S. Lewis. As a scholar of medieval literature, Lewis believed in an inherent hierarchical structure to the universe,[34] a view that assigns levels or roles to every living (and nonliving) thing. According to that view, every being is both "higher" than some and "lower" than others, with the exception of God, who is the highest of all.

Lewis had "a sense of ceremony and hierarchy as being part of the everlasting nature of the world," says one scholar. "Everyone finds oneself in one's proper place."[35] In medieval society, some were emperors; some were queens; some were noblemen and ladies. Others were generals, merchants, scholars, craftsmen, poets, or hardworking farmers. And even though everyone has a different place, the role of the person in power is to care for those under him or her, not to take advantage of them and turn them into servants and underlings.

And that kind of perspective sounds nice and chivalrous in a fairy tale. But to our postmodern ears it has a sinister ring to it. What do you mean some people are "higher" than others? Does that mean they're more valuable? And what does that make *me*? Am I supposed to bow and scrape and pledge fealty to the student body president or something?

Of course not. This isn't saying that some people are of greater *worth* than others. Humans are each equally valuable in the eyes of God. But we are not all equally strong or privileged or born into positions of power. Sin has created enormous inequalities in the social economies of this world. So we have a Kingdom mandate from God to take

care of those who are weaker and more challenged than
we are.

Even though he was Prince of heaven and heir to
God's throne, Jesus himself had no problem rubbing
shoulders with the least important in his society. In fact,
he deliberately sought them out and was found eating
meals with criminals and unrepentant sinners. Even
though he was undoubtedly quite poor himself, he hon-
ored the underprivileged (see Luke 21:1-4), helped the
helpless (see Mark 5:24-34), and restored dignity to the
broken (see Luke 7:36-50). Basically, he treated each person like royalty.

That's because, from God's perspective, every human
being has the dignity and majesty of a king or queen.
We're created to experience the honor and glory of God's
heavenly Kingdom someday, as C. S. Lewis said in his
most famous sermon, "The Weight of Glory." It's important "to remember that the dullest and most uninteresting
person you can talk to may one day be a creature which,
if you saw it now, you would be strongly tempted to worship." Sadly, not everyone will choose the royal destiny

that awaits those who follow Jesus, but even so, Lewis said, "There are no *ordinary* people."[36]

Not only are we created in the image of God, the King of the universe (see Genesis 1:26-27), but we are given the mandate to rule creation as its stewards, taking care of the animals, the plants, and all that God has made (see Genesis 1:28-30). Even more important, as Christians we have the promise from Jesus that we will reign with him someday (see Luke 22:24-30). The weight of kingship is one we carry into eternity.

Meanwhile, we are to act as kings and queens in this life right now: not as those who lord their power over everyone else but as those who use their power to take care of others the way Jesus our King takes care of us. As one author puts it, "Lewis means his readers to take his analogy seriously: just as the Pevensies are children in England and *at the same time* kings and queens in Narnia, so he means us all to live our lives as though we are kings and queens in Narnia."[37] And we might add, as though we are kings and queens of God's Kingdom on earth.

Sure, Peter isn't perfect. He blows up at Edmund, a behavior he later admits probably contributed to the nasty things Edmund did after that. But he realizes where he messed up and admits it to Aslan as soon as possible. He is slowly but surely being made into the person he is meant to be: High King Peter the Magnificent.

We are all meant to be kings and queens who will rule with Christ in his Kingdom someday. Have you claimed the weight of royalty for yourself and others?

Just as my Father has granted me a Kingdom, I now grant you the right to eat and drink at my table in my Kingdom. And you will sit on thrones.

Luke 22:29-30

Further In

- In general, how do you react to those who have "authority over" you?

- How would your behavior toward friends and family change if you were to treat them as fellow kings and queens?

- How does it feel to know that you are royalty in God's eyes?

- What responsibilities do you have as coruler of the earth God has given you? as a fellow monarch alongside the poor and the helpless? toward those who are younger or weaker than you?

- What are you going to do about it?

The Word on Being Royalty

Take some time to read one or more of the following Bible passages:

Psalm 8; Mark 10:35-45; Luke 13:29-30; Romans 5:2; 1 Peter 2:17; 5:2-5

PART SIX
Walking with Narnians

✥

THE LAND BEYOND THE WARDROBE IS FULL OF STRANGE AND
WONDROUS CREATURES, ALL CAUGHT UP IN A DEADLY
STRUGGLE BETWEEN GOOD AND EVIL. LUCY'S ADVENTURE
WITH MR. TUMNUS THE FAUN—AND HIS SUBSEQUENT
ARREST—SENDS THE CHILDREN ON A QUEST TO HELP
THEIR MISSING FRIEND. THEN THEIR CROSS-COUNTRY
FLIGHT WITH THE BEAVERS TAKES THEM DEEP INTO THE
HEART OF A SPELLBOUND REALM, HOPING FOR NEWS OF
THE KING'S RETURN. WHICH SIDE WILL YOU CHOOSE
IN THE BATTLE FOR THE KINGDOM?

To the Rescue

A BASIC PRINCIPLE in search and rescue is that you never, ever put more people at risk in order to save the one.

Or even the nine, as rescue operators discovered in May 2002. On a clear, sunny day, several teams of hikers were attempting to summit formidable, snow-covered Mount Hood in Oregon when the top team lost their footing. They plunged down the mountainside, dragging two other teams with them into a deep crevasse. Three people died. Soon rescue operations were underway for the survivors, many of whom had critical injuries. Then, in a nightmare that made national headlines, a military helicopter sent to retrieve them crashed on the mountainside, injuring one of its crew members and jeopardizing the lives of dozens in the vicinity.[38]

But no one should have been endangered at all. The whole principle behind search and rescue failed, because instead of lives being saved, more people were injured and traumatized.

It's the same dilemma facing Lucy and her siblings when they enter Narnia together and discover that Mr. Tumnus has been arrested by the Witch's Secret Police. He assisted Lucy when she was in potential trouble, so the children feel obligated to go to his rescue somehow. But Mr. Beaver says the best (and only) way to really help their friend is to go to Aslan first. Trying to do it on their own will only lead to more trouble, and possibly to their deaths. He makes a similar statement when Edmund runs off to the White Witch. Peter wants to try and track down his kid brother, but Mr. Beaver knows that would only put them all in greater danger than ever.

Now we must get something straight here: Mr. Beaver's cautionary tone is different from Susan's fearful desire to play it safe. Mr. Beaver knows that Mr. Tumnus and Edmund must be saved. But he also knows that the children aren't the ones to do the saving. Only Aslan can make these situations right in the end. Only the king can do it. Any other plan will lead to danger and even death. Dead heroes aren't much good to anybody.

C. S. Lewis understood heroics. In *Surprised by Joy*, he makes light of a scenario that happened while he was a soldier during World War I. Apparently, he unintentionally stumbled upon a group of sixty or so German soldiers who, it turned out, wanted to surrender. So this young Englishman became a hero by happy accident.[39]

Years later, Lewis undertook very different heroics on behalf of others: prayer. People who knew him remember a man who took the mandate to "never stop praying" (1 Thessalonians 5:17) quite literally. "I don't think I ever came across a person who prayed so much," said Lewis's friend and secretary, Walter Hooper.

"Often in the morning he would get up, go outside to look at the flowers, and stand right there praying. . . . He could pray anywhere and he could compose himself just like he was writing a book. In a train, on a bus, on a walk, or just standing outside. And he prayed on his knees, too, beside his bed."[40]

Lewis believed in the power of prayer to help those in trouble. When Joy Davidman Gresham, the woman he married late in life, was dying of cancer, Lewis asked his friend Father Peter Bide to come to his wife's bedside and lay hands on her and pray. To this day, many believe that her unexpected remission had to do with that prayer. There was certainly no doubt of the connection in Lewis's mind. The doctors could perform all kinds of heroics to save Joy's life, but bringing her into the presence of Jesus the King, through prayer for healing, was the true rescue operation.

Mark 2:1-12 tells how four men came to the rescue of a paralyzed friend in much the same way. When Jesus, the famous healer, visited a house in their village, the crush of people inside and around the house became impenetrable. So the four men put their friend on a mat, climbed up on the roof, dug a hole in the ceiling, and lowered him to Jesus. In short, there was no stopping these guys. It was all or nothing. They knew their friend had no hope without Jesus.

In story after story of the New Testament, we see friends and relatives and children and servants being brought to Jesus for deliverance and healing. There was no such thing as therapy back then. Hospitals hadn't been invented yet. People were desperate. When a friend or family member was in trouble, it affected everyone else too. Jesus offered the only way out.

Today we may not have the privilege of bringing our friends to Jesus in person, but we can bring them to him in prayer. All of us have loved ones who are in real trouble of some kind, who struggle with problems like addiction, depression, or eating disorders. Perhaps they're even in trouble with the law. Whatever their circumstances, it's tempting to try all sorts of heroics on our own to fix the problem. But if we don't first go to Jesus in prayer, we'll only get as far as our own strength takes us before we end up exhausted and eventually give up.

Through prayer, we mentally and spiritually hand our friends over to Jesus' protection and care. We know that they (and we) are being uplifted and empowered by the strength of the King. This doesn't mean everything will go marvelously after that. But we aren't trying to tackle the challenges on our own.

The Beavers know that saving Mr. Tumnus and Edmund is important. It will happen somehow. But they must go to Aslan first. "Once he's with us," Mr. Beaver says of Aslan, "then we can begin doing things."[41]

When your friends are in trouble, you must seek the King's help through prayer instead of trying to rescue them on your own. Will you trust him?

He will continue to rescue us. And you are helping us by praying for us. Then many people will give thanks because God has graciously answered so many prayers for our safety.

2 CORINTHIANS 1:10-11

Further In

• Why is prayer the most important thing you can do for someone who is in a tough situation?

• How tempting is it to try to find a solution to a problem without seeking God's help first?

• Make a list of some things your friends are struggling with (e.g., depression, anxiety, fighting with parents, eating disorders, etc.). Take a moment to pray for each of those situations.

• What would happen if you prayed for your friends on a regular basis?

• What are you going to do about it?

The Word on Coming to the Rescue

Take some time to read one or more of the following Bible passages:

PSALM 17:6-9; JEREMIAH 42:1-4; MARK 9:17-29; EPHESIANS 6:18; PHILIPPIANS 1:19; JAMES 5:13-15; 1 JOHN 5:16-21

Good News

WHEN THE PEVENSIES learn from Mr. and Mrs. Beaver that Aslan is "on the move," it has an effect on all but Edmund "like the first signs of spring, like good news."[42] For the Beavers, the crux of the good news is summed up in the old rhymes and prophecies: "Wrong will be right," when the king returns. And of course that promise sounds great to Peter, Susan, and Lucy—they've sought to do the right thing all along. But for Edmund, who has already decided to head down a wrong path on the side of the White Witch, these prophecies sound more like bad news.

The phrase "good news" has spiritual connotations, as Lewis more than likely recognized. It's the original meaning of the word *gospel*, which comes from the Old English *godspell* or *good spell*, meaning "a good story" or "good news." (Writes J. R. R. Tolkien, "Small wonder that *spell* means both a story told, and a formula of power over living men."[43] Indeed!) For Christians, the good "spell"—the great story, the wonderful news—is that Christ's death and resurrection have saved us from the bad "spell" of sin and death: Those who believe in Jesus are free and forgiven and will spend eternity with God. That's the gospel.

But for C. S. Lewis, when he was a young man and an atheist, this gospel was *not* good news. First, it means that there *is* a God, after all—one who holds us accountable for falling short of his righteous and holy standards. Second, it means that anyone who doesn't side with this God is forever on "the wrong side of the door"[44] of the Kingdom. And finally, even if one does side with this God, it means losing all of one's independence and privacy and personal rights—something the very private Lewis was loath to do. No wonder his writing includes references to God as "the Landlord" (in the allegory *The Pilgrim's Regress*) and as the "transcendental Interferer" (in *Surprised by Joy*). Those are not healthy concepts of who God really is, as Lewis understood once he became a Christian.

Many people can relate to where the pre-Christian Lewis was coming from. They're like the patient in the waiting room who is told by the doctor, "Well, I have some bad news and some good news. The bad news is, you have a disease that will kill you if left untreated. The good news is, there *is* a cure if you're willing to give up your old way of life." If the patient has never before considered that he might be sick and could possibly die, he'll focus on the bad news first. Even the good news sounds bad to him.

The same is true spiritually. Telling others about the Good News of the Kingdom of God may not seem all that great to them at first, but once they grasp that they really are spiritually sick, the cure begins to make sense. Lewis writes, "When you are sick, you will listen to the doctor."[45]

At the beginning of Jesus' ministry, he went to have dinner at the home of Levi (Matthew), along with a bunch of Levi's unscrupulous friends and "other disreputable sinners" (Mark 2:15). The religious leaders couldn't believe that any self-respecting rabbi would sink so low as to eat with "such scum" (verse 16). Jesus' reply hit them right between the eyes: "Healthy people don't need a doctor—sick people do. I have come to call not those who think they are righteous, but those who know they are sinners" (verse 17). The people who were willing to listen to the spiritual diagnosis Jesus had to offer were the ones who knew they had a problem.

And they flocked to him in droves. Many had genuine physical illnesses for which they'd found no cure; to them, Jesus was the Great Physician. And even though he knew that their most deadly disease was a spiritual one, he didn't ignore their physical needs. Yet he often startled them and many onlookers by saying—even as he restored their sight or urged them to get up and walk—that their spiritual illness of sin was healed too. The Good News is bigger than just a refill on our prescription. It is a total spiritual cure.

But people who are not willing to acknowledge their sinfulness or who don't feel guilty about it are going to hear the gospel as a kind of terrifying headline in a bad tabloid newspaper. They may even try to argue you out of the message you're trying to give.

Remember how Edmund questions Mr. Beaver as to which side he's on? And Edmund privately asks Peter if they're really quite sure which *is* the right side to begin with. But it's not an honest question. Edmund knows the right side; he's just chosen against it. So he's trying to steer the issue away from his own sense of guilt and toward whatever proofs or evidence Peter can come up with for choosing the side of the Narnians they've fallen in with.

It's the usual tactic of our nonbelieving friends when we're getting a little too close to their own feelings of guilt, when they don't want to give up the side of selfishness and evil just yet. "Yeah, you think you're so smart? Okay, so prove that your side is the best one. Show me the evidence that God exists. Show me the proof that Jesus really is who he says he is or that you Christians really are headed in the right direction." Meanwhile, they've steered the conversation away from the topic of their own guilt.

So—when you stop and think about it—whether your friend hears the message as good news or bad news depends on what side he or she has already decided to be on.

But there's also the sticky issue of how the message is shared. We've all seen scary sidewalk evangelists screaming at people on street corners and holding up signs that say, "Vengeance is mine, saith the Lord." Who's really listening? Nobody. Because it's bad news. Instead of throwing a life ring to the person who is spiritually drowning, the Bad News Evangelist hollers, "Hey stupid, you're drowning! You're gonna die!" As if the drowning person doesn't know this already. What he really wants is *help*. By contrast, the Good News Evangelist says, "God loves you so much that he's gone to the furthest possible lengths to bring you back to him. Do you want to hear about it?"

Telling people they're messed up and on the losing side is not good news, no matter how you spin it. It may be true, but it's not helpful if you don't tell the other important parts of the story too: that the forces of darkness are not going to have the last word, that the rightful King has returned, that the Kingdom will be restored. Then the hearers can wrestle on their own with whether or not they'll choose the winning side, the side of the King.

We need to claim the Good News that our King is "on the move." Will you share about him in a way that gives hope to others?

This same Good News that came to you is going out all over the world. It is bearing fruit everywhere by changing lives, just as it changed your lives from the day you first heard and understood the truth about God's wonderful grace.

Colossians 1:6

Further In

- Why does the gospel sometimes sound like bad news?

- How easy or difficult is it to convince your nonbelieving friends that the gospel is really good news—without watering down the truth about sin and hell?

- What are some unhelpful ways people try to share about Jesus with others?

- What will it take for some of your friends to really consider where they stand spiritually? What are the different ways you can share the gospel, depending on which friend you're dealing with?

- What are you going to do about it?

The Word on Sharing the Good News

Take some time to read one or more of the following Bible passages:

MATTHEW 4:23-25; MARK 16:15-16; LUKE 4:42-44; ROMANS 10:14-17; 2 CORINTHIANS 2:14-16

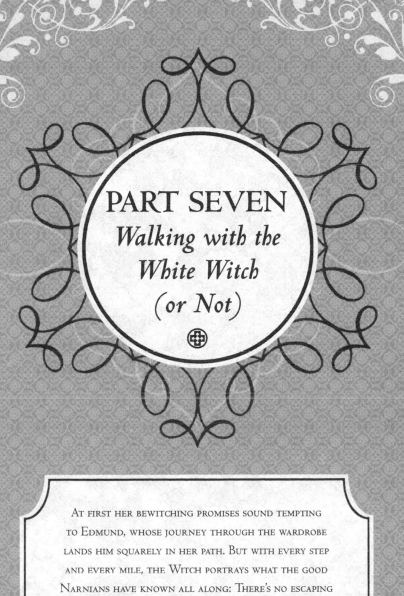

PART SEVEN
Walking with the White Witch (or Not)

AT FIRST HER BEWITCHING PROMISES SOUND TEMPTING
TO EDMUND, WHOSE JOURNEY THROUGH THE WARDROBE
LANDS HIM SQUARELY IN HER PATH. BUT WITH EVERY STEP
AND EVERY MILE, THE WITCH PORTRAYS WHAT THE GOOD
NARNIANS HAVE KNOWN ALL ALONG: THERE'S NO ESCAPING
THE POWERS OF EVIL ONCE YOU'RE CAUGHT. ONLY THE
TRUE KING CAN BREAK THE SPELL.

True Hunger

WHAT'S THE DEAL about the Narnian preoccupation with *food*? In *LWW*, Edmund's first mistake is to eat the White Witch's magic candy. Then once all his siblings have entered Narnia, we hear their practical concerns about supper. Still later, there's considerable time spent on the details of the meal at the Beavers' house. And just wait till we get to *Prince Caspian*! A third of the book focuses on what the Pevensies will find to eat on the deserted island.

Well, some of it could be that Lewis was writing in the midst of a food shortage in England. During World War

II and for a long while afterward, groceries were rationed (e.g., you were only allowed so many sticks of butter per week, per household). With Nazi ships patrolling the surrounding waters, it was a long time before supplies could be transported safely to the islands of Great Britain—and even then, there weren't many supplies to ship. The whole world was reeling in the aftermath of the war.

So Lewis's first generation of readers knew what it was like to go without the stuff they loved to eat. They couldn't walk into their favorite restaurant and order a sizzling steak whenever they wanted. And they couldn't just go down to the local sweetshop and buy . . . oh, say, real imported Turkish delight. For one thing, imports like that were outrageously expensive. Remember, the stuff had to get past enemy subs and aircraft to get there. Even if it was made locally, that didn't help much if the confectioners had run out of sugar.

Puts an interesting spin on Edmund's encounter with the White Witch, doesn't it? It's easy to forget that his life in England takes place during World War II. Maybe— *maybe*—he'll get a taste of his favorite candy at Christmas, but probably never otherwise. He doesn't know what it's like to eat something till it makes you sick. So when the Witch gives him the chance to order anything he wants, he doesn't hesitate: Turkish delight, baby. Bring it on!

It seems hard to believe that anyone would sell his soul (and his siblings) for a bit of candy. But it's a fundamental strategy of evil: The way to a person's soul is through his or her appetites. And we're not just talking about our appetite for food but about all our basic needs: security, contentment, sexual intimacy, companionship, even sleep. Our appetites include every human craving we have.

And these appetites are good things God has given us. They aren't in themselves bad. But when we indulge them, when we become so fixated on them that we can't really focus on anything else, we get derailed from our quest for the Kingdom of God. We become sidetracked by the temporary and lose interest in the eternal. And that's exactly where the devil meets us.

One of C. S. Lewis's most famous works, *The Screwtape Letters*, contains a series of humorous epistles written by a senior demon, Screwtape, to his nephew and underling,

Wormwood. In this highly satiric and imaginative piece of fiction, each junior devil is assigned to a human being (a "patient") in order to create distractions and chaos in that person's life. The goal is to lead the patient away from "the Enemy" (God) and into the clutches of "Our Father Below" (the devil).

Wormwood isn't having the greatest success with his patient, to his uncle's annoyance, so Screwtape offers whatever tips and advice he's learned over the centuries. He especially encourages Wormwood to focus on his patient's appetite for pleasure, namely sex. If he can keep this guy preoccupied with temporal things, Screwtape suggests, then he can keep him from considering eternal realities at all. And, more important, he can lock his patient into an unhealthy cycle of trying to repeat those earthly pleasures, when in fact nothing this side of heaven can ever truly quench human desires. As Screwtape says, "An ever increasing craving for an ever diminishing pleasure is the formula."[46]

The devil almost always makes the appeal to our appetites as his first order of business. Remember the first thing he tempted Jesus with during those forty days of fasting in the desert (see Luke 4:1-13)? "Change this stone into a loaf of bread" (verse 3). Warm, chewy, buttery, delicious bread. Yum, yum, yum. Think *Olive Garden commercial* and you get the idea.

But it was an empty promise, and Jesus knew it. "People do not live by bread alone," he said in reply (verse 4). Our truest hungers and cravings aren't physical at all, but spiritual. We're never truly satisfied without God, no matter what this world might pretend to offer through the glitz and allure of material things.

Edmund soon learns in his adventures with the White Witch that evil doesn't keep its promises. The temptress offers a taste but doesn't deliver. He walks many frigid miles to her palace hoping for more Turkish delight, but all he gets is dry bread. After that, he gets nothing. Instead of magically making food appear, the Witch turns a Christmas feast—along with the people eating it—to stone.

Meanwhile, Edmund's siblings set out for the Stone Table expecting hardship and little food but instead find themselves being offered a feast by Father Christmas and still another by Aslan himself. Then after the final

battle, their king provides a "fine high tea" for every-
body, though where Aslan came up with all that food
isn't quite clear. The point is that he provides. He's
the only one who can truly satisfy the needs of his
people.

Jesus said, "I am the bread of life. Whoever comes to
me will never be hungry again" (John 6:35). If we spend
our days trying to satisfy our earthly appetites, we will
always be disappointed, craving still more and more. But
if we seek after the things of God's Kingdom, we won't
be turned away empty. We will be filled for good, fed by
the King himself.

**Only the legitimate Sovereign can satisfy the
appetites of his people. Will you recognize that,
or will you fall for the devil's empty promises?**

*Temptation comes from our own desires, which entice us and
drag us away. These desires give birth to sinful actions. And
when sin is allowed to grow, it gives birth to death. So don't be
misled, my dear brothers and sisters.*

JAMES 1:14-16

Further In

- How would you feel if you had to go without even a teeny, tiny taste of your favorite food for the next ten years?

- How are our physical appetites connected to our spiritual health? In other words, if you're constantly thinking about your desires for romance or sex or more cool stuff, what does that say about your faith?

- Why does temptation often focus on our physical appetites and desires? How easy or difficult is it for you to resist temptation?

- Why will we never be satisfied without God?

- What are you going to do about it?

The Word on True Hunger

Take some time to read one or more of the following Bible passages:

PSALM 63:1-5; 145:14-16; MARK 14:38; 1 CORINTHIANS 10:12-13; EPHESIANS 5:17-20; 1 JOHN 2:15-17

Deep "Magic"

CHANCES ARE PRETTY GOOD that sometime in your education you've been given a test in which the first line of instructions says, "Read everything on this page before you start." Then there's a bunch of exercises: Multiply this, subtract that, find the square root of such and such, name the capital of Idaho. Then the last line reads, "Now ignore all the above questions, sign your name here, and put your pencil down." D'oh!

If you paid attention to the first rule and did what it said, congratulations. You're smarter than the rest of us.

But if not, like almost everyone else, you marched on through all the exercises, feeling pretty pleased with yourself for being such a dutiful, diligent, instruction-following model student. Until you got to the last line, of course. That's when you discovered that none of the exercises had any bearing on whether or not you passed the test. Had you followed the rules way back at the beginning, you would have known this.

The test is similar to what Aslan is talking about when he says the White Witch may know the Deep Magic—the rules governing the land of Narnia—but she doesn't know the Deeper Magic behind those rules. It's like she began the test partway through and didn't check back to see what the opening instructions had to say. She was following the rules but didn't realize there was a primary rule that would change everything in the end. Imagine what she felt like when she got to the last line and realized she'd flunked!

But of course, the Deep Magic of Narnia is *not* superfluous nonsense, like the test I just described. It's made up of powerful laws from the dawn of time—written in stone, wood, and metal—that must be abided by, or there will be just consequences. That's why the Witch is perfectly within her rights, according to the ancient laws of the Emperor-Beyond-the-Sea, to claim that a traitor's life belongs to her. It's one of the rules, and to break it would be to shatter the foundation of the kingdom itself.

Once again, C. S. Lewis provided an analogy or parable to help us grasp an important spiritual truth. Theologically speaking, when he wrote about the Deep "Magic," what he was talking about was the law—not the human rules put in place by our government in order to keep the peace, but the divine rules God gave his people from the beginning, showing us how to live as citizens of God's holy, righteous Kingdom. When the law is broken, there are appropriate consequences. Justice must be served.

We've heard it all before. God's law requires an accounting for every rule broken; otherwise there's no justice in the universe. Evil actions would go unpunished, and how fair is that? Sin and treachery demand payment. We can't work against this law, nor can we work around it. And we all stand condemned by it, for everyone has broken it at some point or another (see Romans 3:23). No, from the dawn of time to this day, there hasn't been a single person able to make it without breaking God's law.

Except Jesus. The holy Son of God was the only one who could fulfill the requirements of the law. And as such, he paid the penalty of death that we otherwise would have been trying in vain to pay forever.

Funny how it all turns into theological babble the more we try to identify just exactly *what* we're talking about with this whole law business. No wonder C. S. Lewis wrote a story instead! Sure, he tackled the issue of moral law in *Mere Christianity* too. But nothing sticks in our imaginations quite so clearly as the sight of the White Witch, her bare arms raised above her head, standing over the willing, innocent, self-sacrificing Lion on the Stone Table.

As the Witch had hoped, Aslan takes the punishment that Edmund deserves in accordance with the Deep Magic. But Edmund can't possibly foresee that act. Before he meets Aslan face-to-face, he has the same uncomfortable feeling about him that a shoplifter gets when a police officer strolls into the mall. Law enforcement is on the move. The "fun" is over.

And isn't that so often how we perceive the presence of God in our lives? Like some kind of cosmic law enforcement officer who exists primarily to limit our freedoms and make us miserable when we break the rules. As we already mentioned, Lewis himself admitted that as a teenager, he often thought of God as a "transcendental Interferer," a killjoy who was always trying to sabotage what Lewis really wanted to do.

The interesting thing is that both the teenage Lewis and the character Edmund have got it right to some extent: The King really *does* hold us accountable to following the rules of the Kingdom, so he really *is* a kind of cosmic law enforcement officer. But what we fail to grasp is that the King ultimately enforces the law by fulfilling it himself on our behalf. He throws himself into the line of fire, takes the hit, and gives his own life as a ransom during the execution in exchange for ours.

So in the end we are set free—not for anarchy, but to

live the way God requires. We recognize that living by the rules *is* important for this Christian life, just as the newly crowned kings and queens of Narnia still have the mandate to govern justly, establish order, eradicate evil, and stand up for those who are being oppressed. But unlike the Witch, we recognize a Deeper "Magic" at the heart of our actions.

> **The King is the only one who can fulfill the rules he has established for his Kingdom. Will you let him, or sin, have the last word in your life?**

> *The old system under the law of Moses was only a shadow, a dim preview of the good things to come, not the good things themselves.*
> HEBREWS 10:1

Further In

- How easy or difficult is it to live by God's rules?

- Why is it necessary for there to be laws in the Kingdom of God? Why can't we ignore the rules?

- What examples do you see of the consequences

of sin in the lives of people around you? in your own life?

• Why doesn't the law have the last word in our Christian story?

• What are you going to do about it?

The Word on Deep "Magic"

Take some time to read one or more of the following Bible passages:

ISAIAH 53; MATTHEW 5:17-19; 19:23-26; ROMANS 3:20-26; GALATIANS 2:16; HEBREWS 10:11-18

PART EIGHT
Walking with Aslan

❖

THE EVIL SPELL OF WINTER WEAKENS BY THE HOUR,
AND SOON THE RIGHTFUL SOVEREIGN COMES FACE-TO-FACE
WITH THE USURPER. WHILE THE WITCH PLAYS HER PAWN,
THE KING SACRIFICES HIMSELF, AND TO ALL APPEARANCES,
THE GAME IS OVER. BUT THE LION HAS
ONE LAST MOVE . . .

The Great Thaw

As MUCH AS WE might enjoy that new fleece we got for
Christmas or the feel of a groomed slope under our skis,
something inside us eventually begins to tire of bundling
up every time we walk outside. By late winter, a little
warmth from the sun sounds nice. Opening the windows
at school for some fresh air wouldn't be so bad either. A
tiny crocus pushing up through the dead ground would
be a heartening sign. But the sound of running water
would be the best of all, because that would mean the sun
is slowly but surely winning.

From ancient times, spring has been a powerful spiritual metaphor for change and renewal. That's why it
shows up in so many of the great stories, including *The
Lion, the Witch and the Wardrobe.* A land that was lifeless and
hopeless suddenly shows signs of growth. Something big
is about to happen.

The great thaw in *LWW* is directly connected with the
prophecies the Beavers recite about the king's return. As the
thaw turns into spring, the travelers realize that the prophecies aren't just idle nursery rhymes: The stories are coming
true before their very eyes. And if the restoration and
renewal of the land are coming to pass, then certainly all
the promises about the four thrones and the return of
Aslan and the demise of the Witch—those must be
true too!

The Bible tells a similar story. Before Jesus arrived on
the scene, there were hints and signs of his coming. The
Old Testament prophecies spoke of a humble king (see
Zechariah 9:9), a suffering servant (see Isaiah 53), and a
healer who would take care of his people like a shepherd
takes care of a flock (see Isaiah 40:9-11). Specifics were

foretold about the lineage of this ruler—even about his birthplace in Bethlehem (see Micah 5:2). As the Gospel narratives unfold, we see person after person recognizing the signs. God is on the move, just as he promised!

Among the signs was a character by the name of John the Baptist, a distant cousin of Jesus. Before the Savior began his public ministry, John earned celebrity status as an unconventional evangelist in the wilderness outside Jerusalem. People flocked to hear his message of repentance, and many were baptized as a sign of spiritual renewal. Some even began to wonder if John was the one the prophecies were talking about. Luke wrote, "Everyone was expecting the Messiah to come soon, and they were eager to know whether John might be the Messiah" (Luke 3:15). But John set them straight at once. He was merely the messenger God promised to send ahead of the coming Savior (see Luke 3:4-6), just one of the signs that the spiritual thaw had begun.

What happens on a large scale in the New Testament is a macrocosm of what happens in an individual when

God is at work in his or her life. Whenever the Holy Spirit is up to something—whenever God is "on the move"—we are given hints and glimpses of what's about to happen. There are little clues and nudges and signposts along the way.

Ask any Christian who has been on this journey for a while. Most can share about a time when they felt spiritually dead, when spiritual winter had set in. There was no sense of God's presence, no improvement in their circumstances, no personal growth. But then came that random conversation with the guy at the gas station or the book sitting on a friend's coffee table or the guest on that radio show who seemed to speak directly into their soul. Life started stirring like a crocus poking up through the soil. Each little event was a sign, a hint, a clue of something bigger coming just around the corner.

God was definitely up to something in C. S. Lewis's life before the avowed atheist converted to Christianity. Such things don't happen instantaneously. We've already discussed how at one point Lewis felt like he was being offered a choice: He could keep the door of his soul shut or he could open it. And as we mentioned before, he made the choice to open the door *before* he committed his life to Christ. But once he had surrendered that first little bit, he later recalled, he was like a snowman "at long last beginning to melt."[47]

That's why Lewis was able to recognize exactly what was going on in the heart of a young man named Sheldon Vanauken years later. According to Sheldon's memoir, *A Severe Mercy,* he and his wife began to explore the truths of Christianity while studying at the University of Oxford. There Sheldon found himself asking spiritual questions he'd never seriously considered before. He wrote to Lewis, since the Oxford don seemed like an intelligent Christian who would give him a straight answer. And Lewis did. "The Holy Spirit is after you," he wrote back. "I doubt if you'll get away!"[48] Of course, that wasn't really what Sheldon wanted to hear, but it wasn't long before he surrendered to Christ anyway.

Theologians through the centuries have tried to find ways to express this kind of preconversion experience. The eighteenth-century founder of the Methodist move-

ment, John Wesley, called it prevenient grace: God is at
work in your life before you're even conscious of him (as
opposed to the word *convenient*, like the 7-Eleven that
shows up just as you're conscious you'd like a Slurpee).
Through the lens of prevenient grace, you look back and
realize all the ways God has been there—taking care of
you in the midst of that awful car accident, for example,
or prompting you to sign up for that theology class. He
was "on the move," even though you didn't recognize him
at the time.

Perhaps lately a friend or family member has been
asking questions about faith when previously they
seemed to have no interest in it. Be careful that you
don't dismiss what's happening as "just a phase" they're
going through. They never would be asking unless
God was beginning to thaw the frozen parts of their
soul. Such questions are like the trickle, trickle, trickle
of running water when there was nothing but solid
ice before. It's your clue that something big is
going on.

Not just a thaw, but *spring!*

When the King returns to his rightful throne, all signs point to the healing and restoration of the Kingdom. What are the hints in your life or the lives of others that the King is on the move?

I am about to do something new. See, I have already begun! Do you not see it?
Isaiah 43:19

Further In

- What are some ways God might be trying to get your attention?

- When you sense that God is on the move in your life, are you excited or annoyed?

- What are some signs that God is at work in the lives of your friends—without them even being aware of it?

- What will it take to melt their hearts?

- What are you going to do about it?

The Word on Renewal

Take some time to read one or more of the following Bible passages:

PSALM 65:9-13; ISAIAH 35:1-7; LUKE 21:29-33; ROMANS 8:19-25; REVELATION 21:1-7

Deeper "Magic"

THE SUN PEEPS over the horizon, the Stone Table gives a mighty crack, and Aslan is miraculously, joyfully *alive*. But how is this possible? What happened to the Deep Magic?

After Aslan's return from death, C. S. Lewis provides in a few short sentences an explanation for both Aslan's resurrection and Edmund's redemption that somehow satisfies the child reader in us: The Witch didn't know there was a Deeper Magic from before the dawn of time that would reverse all the evil she intended. But in our own Christian story, the concepts of resurrection and redemption are terribly complex. It's no simple discussion why Jesus' sacrifice is the final answer to the problem of sin in the world and how death itself begins working "backward" as a result. Suffice it to say that Lewis has captured a little of how God's Kingdom operates by introducing the concept of a first and older "rule" at its very center.

And what is this rule, this Deeper "Magic"? *Love*. Not affection, not friendship, not sexual attraction, but *agape*: the compassionate, selfless love God has for us when we're at our most unlovable. Lewis called it "charity" in his book *The Four Loves* (the original meaning of that word has changed over the years, unfortunately). It's the highest and holiest kind of love, straight from God's heart.

But such love is difficult to accept. We assume that we're the object of God's love because there's something inherently adorable or good or endearing about us that God finds irresistible. Not so. Lewis says, "Christ did not die for men because they were intrinsically worth dying for, but because He is intrinsically love, and therefore loves infinitely."[49] God loves because it's the very definition of who he is (see I John 4:8).

There's no getting around it. No matter how peevish or cruel or rebellious we are, God is bound by his very nature to love us. That's the first rule of his Kingdom, grounded in his character.

Think of it in terms of Aslan's treatment of Edmund. Edmund has made himself about as unlovable as a storybook character can get. From the beginning he's been a grumbler, a tease, a liar, a skeptic, and ultimately a traitor. The last thing he deserves is to be rescued from the Witch's clutches, to be delivered from the enemy with whom he sided *on purpose*. Still less does he deserve to be saved at such a high cost. Yet none of this has any bearing on what Aslan has already chosen to do. Before Edmund's rescue and consequent apologies to those he betrayed, Aslan says to Lucy, "All shall be done."[50] We get the impression that he has always intended to save Edmund, long before Edmund knew he needed saving.

Shortly before his death Jesus said, "There is no greater love than to lay down one's life for one's friends" (John 15:13). It's a wonderful image: a close-knit band of soldiers, pledging to stick by their best friends through thick and thin. But let's consider who Jesus' friends were. There was Matthew the tax collector, considered slime by the rest of society. There's Judas the traitor, definitely a liability. Thomas the skeptic was among them as well, along with Peter, who also struggled to take Jesus at his word. Later Peter would deny ever knowing him. In the end, every last one fled from the scene of Jesus' execution. And *this* was the lousy band of brothers God died for?

Yep. And we're all included in that rabble, whether we like it or not. The Bible makes it pretty clear: "Most people would not be willing to die for an upright person, though someone might perhaps be willing to die for a person who is especially good. But God showed his great love for us by sending Christ to die for us while we were still sinners" (Romans 5:7-8). Because God is God, he has loved us from the beginning, but we didn't truly grasp it until Jesus came and demonstrated *agape* once and for all.

Too often we get caught up in trying to earn—or in thinking we deserve—God's approval rather than realizing that we, like Edmund, have been saved in spite of ourselves. In fact, our *selves* don't have much say in the matter, other than surrendering to God in utter gratitude. We could ignore his free gift. We often do, thinking we still have to work, work, work for it, thinking we're still intrinsically lovable somehow. But as Edmund knows, there's nothing to be done but take our gaze off of self and fix our eyes on the King.

In walking with Aslan, Edmund makes the seismic shift from self-love to *agape* love. That's why he's able to give no thought to himself in the battle against the White Witch but instead drives through enemy lines till he's within reach of her wand. He's willing to sacrifice himself if need be for the sake of all Narnia.

You, too, are called to love others till it hurts, till it costs you something. And that isn't limited to the people you naturally feel drawn to, like your friends and family. It includes those who, like Edmund, have made themselves just about as unlovable as they can possibly be. Yet through your selfless grace and compassion, they can receive a glimpse of the true King.

Agape love is the Deeper "Magic" at the heart of God's Kingdom. Where would you be without it?

When God our Savior revealed his kindness and love, he saved us, not because of the righteous things we had done, but because of his mercy.
TITUS 3:4-5

Further In

- Why do so many people have a hard time accepting God's *agape* love for them?

- How easy is it for you to get so wrapped up in going your own selfish way—or, on the flip side, trying to follow all the rules—that you forget how much God loves you?

- How will you treat others with *agape*, especially when they're not particularly lovable?

- What are you willing to give up for them?

- What are you going to do about it?

The Word on God's Love for Us

Take some time to read one or more of the following Bible passages:

DEUTERONOMY 7:7-9; NEHEMIAH 9:16-21; PSALM 103; GALATIANS 2:19-21; 5:13-14; 1 JOHN 4:7-11

PART NINE
Walking with Lewis

✠

As we've discovered by now, it's not easy keeping up with one of the greatest fantasy authors of all time. He outstrips most of us in both intellect and imagination. But with each step, we find ourselves further in and still further in to the mysteries of faith. And the quest isn't over yet! Better hike up your jeans, tie your shoes, and grab a snack for the road.

The Open Door

WE CAN'T GO FAR in any fantasy story without stumbling upon doors that lead to the unknown.

Think about *The Lord of the Rings*: Remember the magic entrance to the Mines of Moria in *The Fellowship of the Ring*? Or the freaky doorway to the Paths of the Dead in *The Return of the King*? ("The way is shut!" Shiver . . .) Classic literature is full of passageways and portals and mysterious keys that unlock who-knows-what. There's even a magic wardrobe in a short story by Edith Nesbit entitled "The Aunt and Amabel" (or "Anabel"), published in

1912 as part of the collection *The Magic World.* C. S. Lewis was known to read and enjoy Nesbit's works, and some scholars believe they might have influenced his imagination over the years.[51]

It could be. But the open or unlocked door is a critical prop in many fairy tales and has been a timeless symbol in myths and legends for centuries. Lewis was masterfully following in the footsteps of great storytellers who knew exactly how to pique our curiosity and hook us at the opening scene—and keep us guessing till the closing pages.

If we walk very far with our beloved author, we soon discover that the entrances into and out of his imaginary world are as many and varied as his characters themselves. There's the little door to the attic room in *The Magician's Nephew* as well as the exit out of Narnia at the end of *Prince Caspian.* There's the hallway full of doors at the wizard's house in *The Voyage of the "Dawn Treader"* and the gate in the wall at Jill and Eustace's school in *The Silver Chair.* And we can't forget the entrance to the stable at the end of *The Last Battle.*

But first Lucy finds the wardrobe door unlocked in the opening scene of *The Lion, the Witch and the Wardrobe*, and so all the Narnia adventures begin.

As most authors of fantasy stories are well aware, the open or unlocked door is a powerful symbol for entering the world of the spirit, the Kingdom beyond the world we know. We've already discussed how we long to see this Kingdom, to be welcomed into the presence of the King. But we're not always sure how to find the door, if it exists at all, and we're not necessarily confident that anyone will answer us when we knock.

Give it a shot, Jesus tells his followers. The door is there. "Keep on knocking, and the door will be opened," he says (Luke 11:9). And how does he know? Well, not only is he the King who calls and welcomes us to his country, but he *is* the door. "Yes, I am the gate," Jesus says. "Those who come in through me will be saved" (John 10:9). There are no adventures in the land of faith till we recognize that Jesus is the door we've been looking for all along.

Wait a minute. Haven't we always heard there are *many* doors to God? People of various worldviews and backgrounds—including some well-meaning but misinformed Christians—insist that you can get in any way you please, even through paganism or cults or Eastern meditation. And certainly God will set our hearts longing for the Kingdom in whatever way he can, using whatever chinks and cracks he finds in the hard shell of our souls. But there's a difference between longing for the Kingdom and actually getting there. If we take Jesus' words seriously, there's no detour around what he had to say about himself: "I am the way, the truth, and the life. No one can come to the Father except through me" (John 14:6). Chinks and cracks may let in a little light, but the open door is the only way out of prison into the sunshine.

But, someone might argue, aren't there lots of doors into and out of Narnia? So isn't Lewis saying that there are lots of ways to enter the Kingdom? Well, there may be many portals to the otherworld of Narnia, but the one thing all those doors have in common is Good "Magic." There's some kind of good power at work, calling and chasing the characters into or out of the land of adventure. In fact, we can say that the doors only function as portals between the worlds because Aslan makes them so. He creates a way where there wasn't a way before. The king is the key; and so it is with faith.

By the end of Lewis's story, we've almost forgotten the wardrobe. It doesn't occur to us till the closing pages that the entrance into Narnia is also the exit back to the real world of daily responsibilities. Even after the children have grown into young women and men, kings and queens of the land, the door is still there, waiting in the woods of Lantern Waste for the return of the travelers who stumbled through it so many years ago.

And so we realize that the lessons we learn on the quest in the Kingdom are meant to be applicable in ordinary, everyday life. We come back to our daily existence having been changed by our time spent in the presence of the King, acutely aware that we don't get to stay in his presence forever—not yet. There's work to be done on this side of the door until time itself draws to a close and we are reunited with Jesus in his Kingdom.

So back through the door we go, into whatever adventures God has for us next in the real world, waiting for the day when he calls us to be with him.

The door to the Kingdom is unlocked and waiting. Will you give it a try?

I have opened a door for you that no one can close.
REVELATION 3:8

Further In

- If you haven't yet acknowledged Jesus as the true door to knowing God, what's holding you back?

- Where might your quest through the door of faith take you next?

- What doors are being left open for you to bring the lessons of the Kingdom into your everyday life? (Consider your friend who asks questions about faith or the opportunity to go on a mission trip during spring break.)

- What work have you been given to do on this

side of the door while you wait for your King's return?

• What are you going to do about it?

The Word on Opening the Door

Take some time to read one or more of the following Bible passages:

PSALM 24:7-10; MATTHEW 7:13-14; 16:13-19; LUKE 13:24-25; 2 PETER 1:10-11; REVELATION 3:20-21

Further In

HAVE YOU EVER NOTICED how the last scene of *The Lion, the Witch and the Wardrobe* so eerily echoes the first? Both episodes find the Pevensie siblings on an adventure beyond the borders of the world they know, and both times they take the plunge further in.

At the beginning of the story, before Lucy discovers the magical powers of the wardrobe, the children are on the hunt for fun. They're determined to explore all the nooks and crannies of the Professor's estate: the endless rooms inside as well as the trackless wood outside. And all that sounds exciting enough the first time we read or watch the opening scene. A funky old house in the country, full of mysterious rooms, and almost no adult supervision? Cool. Little do we know the *real* adventure C. S. Lewis has planned!

Within just a few pages, Lucy finds the wardrobe door unlocked. But she doesn't stop there. She climbs inside. She takes "a step further in," and then another and another—"still further in"—until she pushes through the walls of this world into an extraordinary country. Needless to say, those silly games of hide-and-seek were mere child's play. This is the real thing.

Many, many adventures later, Lucy and her grown siblings are at it again, except this time they're on the hunt for the White Stag. All the mysteries of the Professor's wooded estate, back in the dim past of their childhood, have been utterly forgotten. Even the lamp-post looks strange. But again—as they did that first time—they dare to take the next step beyond the familiar, going further in and still further in till there's no turning back.

The phrase "further in" is not accidental to *LWW*, nor is it limited to this particular work of Lewis's. Not only does it show up again later in the story (when Mr. Beaver invites the children to "come further in" so they won't be over-heard) but for readers of *The Chronicles of Narnia*, it's language we hear again toward the end of *The Last Battle*, when the Narnians are invited to come "further up and further in" to the mountains of Aslan's country. The same turn of phrase also appears in *The Great Divorce* as well as in a more obscure essay, "Modern Translations of the Bible," from Lewis's *God in the Dock*.[52] Who would have guessed two little words could come loaded with so much meaning?

The thrust of the phrase is about daring to take the next step. It's a concept we see in many fantasy stories. Often the characters set out on their quests from the very edges of the known world—the Western Wilds of Lantern Waste in Narnia or the "far downs" of the Shire in Middle-earth, for example—and they must make their way beyond the borders of their personal experience into a foreign land. If they don't take the next step, they won't have much of a journey. And if there's no journey, the characters won't stumble upon any adventures. And if there aren't any adventures, then it's a story not worth telling.

Perhaps that's why fantasy stories make such great metaphors for faith. Faith is also a journey further in. It takes us somewhere. It may not be a physical journey from point A to point B (though some folks find themselves being sent to the far-flung reaches of the earth). But it does require us to move from our kindergarten picture books about Jesus, for example, to personal study of the Bible itself. Yes, we *are* smart enough to understand that book, with God's help. Too often we pretend we don't get what Jesus is talking about because we're too chicken to do what he says. We're not willing to go further in.

And yet that's exactly what Jesus challenges his followers to do. "Follow me," Jesus said to a stranger named Levi (otherwise known as Matthew), and we read that "Levi got up, left everything, and followed him" (Luke 5:27-28). Elsewhere, when Jesus said "follow me" to a young man who claimed to be seeking eternal life (Matthew 19:21), the young man wasn't willing to take the next step. Others asked to follow Jesus but then insisted on taking care of things back home first. Jesus replied,

"Anyone who puts a hand to the plow and then looks back is not fit for the Kingdom of God" (Luke 9:62). The King isn't interested in halfhearted attempts.

A concerted effort to walk with Jesus will take us even deeper in our journey of faith, moving us from apathy to passion, fear to trust, disobedience to obedience, cynicism to joy. Oswald Chambers wrote, "If things are dark to me, then I may be sure there is something I will not do."[53] If we're feeling spiritually stuck, there's some step we are refusing to take. Perhaps we've hurt a friend by our unkind words but we can't let down our pride and apologize. Or maybe we feel like God is telling us to help someone financially but we secretly think that person isn't "worthy." More often, we fail to act on the simple things, like setting the alarm to get up for church on Sunday morning.

But once we get past our stubbornness, another landscape opens up before us, leading to new adventures of faith that we never would have had if we hadn't taken those initial steps. We meet someone new at church; we see the dignity and joy on the face of the one who needed the financial aid; we realize just how much our estranged friend really meant to us after all. The next steps get easier and easier until going back seems less and less appealing. After all, it's harder to turn back from the quest for the Kingdom when you've gone a good distance inside its borders, which is, of course, exactly what God wants.

You (or a friend) may be one of those people standing on the threshold of faith, looking in. Fine. Great. That's better than being nowhere near the open door. But once you're on the threshold, eventually it will be time to take some steps further inside. If you really want to embark on the quest, you can't just say, "Hey, there's an open door!" and then turn around and walk away. The real adventure of faith begins *after* you turn the handle and pass into whatever lies beyond.

That's the invitation Lewis extends to us. He challenges his readers to go further into the Kingdom of God by taking the next step, whether or not we're really sure where the journey is taking us. The King brooks no nonsense; he accepts no whining or excuses. He expects our journey to change and mature us. We don't get to stay in spiritual kindergarten. That's because we're like eggs, Lewis says. "We must be hatched or go bad."[54]

You're invited on a journey further in to the adventure of faith. Will you take the next step, whatever that might be?

I focus on this one thing: Forgetting the past and looking forward to what lies ahead, I press on to reach the end of the race and receive the heavenly prize for which God, through Christ Jesus, is calling us.

Philippians 3:13-14

Further In

- What are the ways you can go "further in" with your faith in God?

- What keeps you from taking those steps?

- When are you tempted to turn around and go back? What are the consequences? What will keep you on the journey?

- How can you encourage your friends to go "further in" with their walk with Jesus? How can they encourage *you*?

• What are you going to do about it?

The Word on Going Further In
Take some time to read one or more of the following Bible passages:

PROVERBS 4:25-27; ISAIAH 30:20-21; MATTHEW
10:38-39; LUKE 9:57-62; JOHN 12:26; 1 PETER 1:6

READ THIS LAST

It seems like we've only just begun our quest, and here we are already at the closing thoughts of this particular Narnia adventure. After all, C. S. Lewis was the master at keeping things short and to the point. But there are more tales to come, and if we stick to the spiritual path our beloved author encouraged us to take, we'll discover a lifetime of wisdom to keep us company along the way.

Meanwhile, here are some final thoughts on what our quest for the Kingdom is meant to accomplish in our lives, gleaned from what the Pevensies themselves learn while walking with Aslan.

Peter, the eldest and the future high king, spends time with the Lion alone, surveying the land he will lead one day and going over the battle plan for war against evil. Through walking with Aslan, he learns to recognize danger when he sees it and to take immediate action. He wasn't given a sword and shield by Father Christmas for nothing! From now on, the forces of darkness won't have the last word.

Edmund, the rebel-traitor, also spends time with Aslan alone after being rescued from the Witch. No one but Edmund knows what he and the Lion discussed that morning, but when it's over, Edmund is transformed from a self-centered schoolboy into a humble but stouthearted young king. Noble obedience has replaced squirming rebellion, and through it Edmund becomes who he was meant to be all along.

Susan has a sad journey at Aslan's side: She walks with the Lion in his suffering and feels the pity and despair about all that takes place on the Stone Table. It's a grief too deep for words. In experiencing the depths of Aslan's sorrow, she grasps the heights of his compassion. She recognizes what true love has cost her king and thus will serve the people he died for with gentleness and mercy.

Lucy, too, walks with Aslan in his suffering, but she also experiences the transforming joy of his resurrection when the sun rises and the Table cracks and he stands before them, alive! Surprise and delight overpower her at the sight of her risen lord; she can't contain her laughter. And Aslan doesn't insist on solemnity at this moment. Instead, he joins in the fun—he *creates* the fun! In walking with Aslan—running, riding, flying—Lucy is caught up in the comedy of it all, the happy ending no one could have anticipated. She learns how to hope even in the darkest moments and to serve others with joy.

In the end, every quality the Pevensies gain as marks of royalty—magnificence, justice, gentleness, valiance—are characteristics of Aslan himself. Even though we see hints of these virtues latent inside each child from the opening scenes, it isn't until they've spent significant time in the Lion's presence that these qualities become the most defining characteristics of their lives. Walking with the king makes them more like him.

It's the same kind of spiritual transformation God works in each of us as we spend time with our Lord. We walk with Jesus in battle and become trained in how to fight evil and injustice in this dark world. We follow him in obedience and soon discover his true purpose for our lives. We cling to his side through suffering, learning compassion for others. And we celebrate the joy of his resurrection, gaining delight in the Kingdom work we've been given while waiting with hope for his return.

So this is where our quest through the wardrobe of faith ultimately leads us. It's not just about having one cool adventure after another, but about becoming more like the King we pledge to serve. Then in the midst of our everyday routine, we can live more truly as the kings and queens he wants us to be.

> *We ask God to give you complete knowledge of his will and to give you spiritual wisdom and understanding. Then the way you live will always honor and please the Lord, and your lives will produce every kind of good fruit. All the while, you will grow as you learn to know God better and better.*
>
> COLOSSIANS 1:9-10

GLOSSARY OF TERMS & FUN FACTS

RELATED TO C. S. LEWIS AND *The Lion, the Witch and the Wardrobe*

ASLAN   The king of Narnia, a great Lion. He offers his life to the White Witch in exchange for that of the traitor Edmund but returns from the dead to defeat her. [Fun fact: The word *aslan* means "lion" in Turkish.[55]]

BEAVERS   Two talking beasts of Narnia, husband and wife, who shelter Peter, Susan, Edmund, and Lucy after the children learn of Mr. Tumnus's arrest.

CAIR PARAVEL   The Narnian castle on the sea where four thrones await the coming of two Sons of Adam and two Daughters of Eve.

CAMBRIDGE*   The university in England where

---

* Having to do with stuff in the real world rather than the world of Narnia

C. S. Lewis taught medieval and Renaissance literature.

DAUGHTER OF EVE   A title used by Narnians in reference to a female human being.

EDMUND   The third child in the Pevensie family and the most skeptical. He betrays his siblings to the White Witch, but after his transformation from bad to good, he becomes King Edmund the Just.

FATHER CHRISTMAS   The British name for Santa Claus; his appearance in Narnia is the first clear sign that the spell of the White Witch is weakening. He gives Peter, Susan, and Lucy gifts to aid them in the tasks ahead.

GREAT KNOCK, THE* (1848–1921)   Lewis's nickname for W. T. Kirkpatrick (also known as "Kirk"), his private tutor for several years of high school and the one who taught him how to apply logic and reason to every argument.

GRESHAM, JOY DAVIDMAN* (1915–1960)   The American poet whom C. S. Lewis married late in life, to everyone's surprise. They were married only a few short years before Joy died after a valiant battle with cancer.

INKLINGS, THE* A group of British scholars and writers made up of C. S. Lewis, J. R. R. Tolkien, Charles Williams, Owen Barfield, and others, who met weekly (sometimes twice a week) near Oxford during the 1930s and 1940s to read and critique each other's works.

JADIS See *White Witch*.

LAMP-POST The first thing Lucy sees when she enters the land of Narnia through the wardrobe. It stands lit in the middle of a snowy wood.

LEWIS, C. S.* (1898–1963) Author of *The Chronicles of Narnia* and other celebrated works of both fiction and nonfiction; considered by many to be the greatest Christian author of the twentieth century. Born in Ireland and educated in England, he eventually made his home in Oxford as a scholar and tutor of literature. He converted from atheism to Christianity as a young man; he married late in life but had no children of his own. [Fun fact: Lewis's self-appointed nickname was "Jack" (originally "Jacksie"), a name he decided upon as a small child that stuck with him for the rest of his life. Would *you* want to be known forever as "Clive Staples"? Didn't think so.]

LOTR*   Customary shorthand for *The Lord of the Rings.*

LOTR JUNKIES*   *The Lord of the Rings* fanatics who host their own fan-sites, talk like Orlando Bloom, and recite the Pledge of Allegiance in Elvish.

LUCY   The youngest of the four Pevensie children and the first to get into Narnia from our world. She is the most trusting of the four and eventually earns the name Queen Lucy the Valiant. [Fun fact: Lucy is named after a real girl named Lucy Barfield, to whom *The Lion, the Witch and the Wardrobe* is dedicated; she's the daughter of Owen Barfield (see *Inklings*) and one of Lewis's godchildren.]

LWW Customary shorthand for *The Lion, the Witch and the Wardrobe.*

MACDONALD, GEORGE* (1824–1905) Scottish minister and author whose fantasy works impressed C. S. Lewis. Some of his stories include *Phantastes, Lilith, The Golden Key, At the Back of the North Wind,* and *The Princess and the Goblin.*

MACREADY, MRS. The housekeeper of the Professor's large estate in the country.

NARNIA The magical otherworld that Lucy Pevensie discovers beyond the wardrobe where beasts can talk and a Lion is the true king. For a hundred years it's been under the rule of the evil White Witch, who has made it perpetual winter. It is the task of the Pevensie children to set the land free with the help of Aslan. [Fun fact: There is a real village in the central part of Italy called Narni whose ancient Roman name was Narnia. Coincidentally(?), next to the cathedral in the village is a shrine to a local saint, "Blessed Lucy of Narnia!"[56]]

OXFORD* The university in England where C. S.
   Lewis tutored for many years; the town where he
   made his home.

PETER The eldest of the Pevensie children and the
   quickest to take action when something needs to be
   done. He becomes High King Peter, also known as
   Peter the Magnificent.

PEVENSIE The last name of the four English children
   who discover the magical land of Narnia. They are
   sent to a large house in the country to avoid the
   bombing of London during World War II, and it is
   through an old wardrobe in the house that they
   enter Narnia. [Fun fact: C. S. Lewis, himself an
   English professor, sheltered children in his home
   during the air raids.]

PROFESSOR, THE Owner of the English house in the
   country where the Pevensie children are guests. It is
   he who first believes Lucy's story about Narnia—
   probably because he has his own Narnia story to
   tell. (You can read about it in *The Magician's Nephew*.)

SON OF ADAM A title used by Narnians in reference to male human beings.

STONE TABLE An ancient carved platform where the children first meet Aslan; the location of the Lion's execution by the White Witch.

SUSAN The second-eldest of the Pevensie children and the most cautious. Through her adventures in Narnia she earns the title Queen Susan the Gentle.

TOLKIEN, J. R. R.* (1892–1973) Celebrated author of *The Hobbit* and *The Lord of the Rings* and a good friend of C. S. Lewis. He was a central member of the Inklings and was instrumental in Lewis's conversion from atheism to Christianity. [Fun fact: Tolkien often said that he might never have finished *LOTR* if it hadn't been for the constant encouragement of C. S. Lewis.[57]]

TRILEMMA A problem in which there are only three possible solutions (as opposed to a dilemma, in which there are two possible solutions). The Professor poses a trilemma to Peter and Susan when discussing Lucy's claim to have visited Narnia.

TUMNUS THE FAUN　Also known as Mr. Tumnus; the first character Lucy meets in Narnia. He's supposed to turn her over to the White Witch but helps her escape instead, and as a result, he's arrested and turned to stone.

WARDROBE　The entrance to the magical world of Narnia from a spare room in the Professor's house in England. [Fun fact: C. S. Lewis himself owned an intricately carved wardrobe that is now on display at the Marion E. Wade Center at Wheaton College in Illinois. The image on the cover of this book is a picture of that wardrobe, taken with the permission of the Wade Center.]

WETA GEEKS*　Fans of the digital and visual movie effects created by Weta Workshop (see below).

WETA WORKSHOP*　The New Zealand company behind the visual and digital effects in *The Lord of the Rings* and *The Chronicles of Narnia* movies.

WHITE WITCH, THE　Also known as Jadis; an evil queen who put the wintry spell on Narnia. She holds Edmund hostage but agrees to give him up in exchange for Aslan's life, thinking she is victorious. But she is defeated when Aslan returns from the dead.

WOLVES   Not always evil; some of them are employed as secret police of the White Witch. Peter fights his first battle when he kills Fenris Ulf (or Maugrim), the Wolf Captain.

GUIDE TO OTHER WORKS BY C. S. LEWIS

Now is a great time to dive "further in" to some of Lewis's other works while you're waiting for the next Narnia movie. (The lists below are merely a sampling of his stuff.) Perhaps you're curious about the cutting wit of *The Screwtape Letters*. Or maybe you're intrigued by the bizarre bus ride of *The Great Divorce*. Or if you're looking for more of the one-two punch of his nonfiction Christian apologetics, *Mere Christianity* is a corker. Whatever the case, you're sure to find something on this list that piques your interest.

NARNIA FICTION BY C. S. LEWIS
This author recommends that you read *The Chronicles of Narnia* in the order in which they were originally published:

> *The Lion, the Witch and the Wardrobe*
> *Prince Caspian*
> *The Voyage of the "Dawn Treader"*

The Silver Chair

The Horse and His Boy

The Magician's Nephew

The Last Battle

[Fun fact: All seven books have been made into excellent audio dramas by Focus on the Family's Radio Theatre, complete with an award-winning cast and cinema-quality sound design and music (Tyndale House Publishers). Two thumbs up (and both big toes too) from this author!]

OTHER FICTION BY C. S. LEWIS

The Space Trilogy, which includes *Out of the Silent Planet*, *Perelandra*, and *That Hideous Strength* — Lewis's science fiction series. [Fun fact: *The Space Trilogy* was written as the result of an agreement between Lewis and Tolkien: Lewis would write a space travel series, and Tolkien would write a time travel series.[58] Needless to say, *LOTR* kept Tolkien busy for so many decades that he never got around to it (maybe that's where the time travel part came in!).]

The Screwtape Letters — Notes from a senior demon, Screwtape, to his nephew and underling, Wormwood, offering advice on how to keep his assigned human "patient" under control.

The Great Divorce — A bizarre bus ride from hell to heaven and what the travelers find once they get there. Lewis makes the case that heaven and hell are completely divorced from each other: We can't keep going down the wrong road hoping it leads to the right place eventually.

Till We Have Faces: A Myth Retold — A beautiful and poignant retelling of the Greek myth of Cupid and Psyche, told from the standpoint of Psyche's sister Orual.

NONFICTION BY C. S. LEWIS

Mere Christianity — Originally a series of radio broadcasts given by Lewis on the BBC during World War II, it's considered one of the most intelligent and eloquent arguments in defense of Christianity ever written.

Surprised by Joy: The Shape of My Early Life — Lewis's autobiographical memoir of his childhood and youth, largely focused on his conversion from atheism to Christianity. [Fun fact: Joy was also the name of the woman Lewis married late in life, several years after the publication of this book.]

The Four Loves — A discussion of the four kinds of love: affection, friendship, sexual attraction, and *agape*, or the self-sacrificing love God has toward us.

C. S. Lewis: Letters to Children, edited by Lyle Dorsett and Marjorie Lamp Mead (Simon & Schuster, 1995) — A wonderful collection of some of Lewis's letters to friends, fans, and godchildren. [Fun fact: Lewis made it a priority to respond to every single letter he ever received.]

God in the Dock, selected essays, including "Myth Became Fact," "The Grand Miracle," and "What Are We to Make of Jesus Christ?" — Powerful arguments in defense of the Christian worldview. [Fun fact: This has nothing to do with boating! The word *dock* is a British term used in a court of law to indicate the place where the witness or defendant stands when asked to testify.]

OTHER STUFF ABOUT C. S. LEWIS

Companion to Narnia: A Complete Guide to the Enchanting World of C. S. Lewis's The Chronicles of Narnia, by Paul F. Ford

(HarperCollins, 1994) — A complete encyclopedia of names and concepts related to Narnia.

Finding God in the Land of Narnia, by Kurt Bruner and Jim Ware, best-selling authors of *Finding God in The Lord of the Rings* (both by Tyndale House Publishers) — Reflections on some of the spiritual themes in *The Chronicles of Narnia*.

The Magic Never Ends: The Life and Work of C. S. Lewis — The only full-length documentary on C. S. Lewis: narrated by Sir Ben Kingsley, produced by the Duncan Group and Crouse Entertainment, and aired on PBS. There's also a companion book of the same name by John Ryan Duncan (W Publishing Group, 2001). [Fun fact: There's no film footage of Lewis known to be in existence, and only a few dozen photographs have surfaced since his death. Imagine creating a full-length documentary out of *that!*]

Shadowlands — A major motion picture starring Anthony Hopkins and Debra Winger (1993); depicts the love story between Lewis and the woman he married late in life, the American writer Joy Davidman Gresham. Grab your Kleenex!

The Quotable Lewis, edited by Wayne Martindale and Jerry Root (Tyndale House Publishers) – A handy reference guide of quotes by Lewis, arranged in alphabetical order by topic.

That should keep you busy enough for a while!

NOTES

1. From C. S. Lewis's introduction to *Lilith* by George MacDonald (Grand Rapids, Mich.: William B. Eerdmans Publishing Company, 1981), xi.

2. C. S. Lewis, *Surprised by Joy* (New York: Harvest Books, 1966), chapter 11; C. S. Lewis, *The Great Divorce* (New York: HarperCollins, 2001), chapter 9; and the introduction to *Lilith*, xii.

3. John Ryan Duncan, *The Magic Never Ends: The Life and Work of C. S. Lewis* (Nashville: W Publishing Group, 2001), chapter 3.

4. J. R. R. Tolkien, *The Tolkien Reader* (New York: Ballantine Books, 1966), 88–89.

5. Wayne Martindale and Jerry Root, eds., *The Quotable Lewis* (Wheaton, Ill.: Tyndale House Publishers, 1989), 444.

6. Tolkien, *The Tolkien Reader*, 67.

7. Martindale and Root, *The Quotable Lewis*, 90.

8. Duncan, *The Magic Never Ends*, 84–85.

9. C. S. Lewis, "Rejoinder to Dr. Pittenger" in *God in the Dock* (Grand Rapids, Mich.: William B. Eerdmans Publishing Company, 1970), 183.

10. Leland Ryken, ed., *The Christian Imagination: The Practice of Faith in Literature and Writing* (Colorado Springs: WaterBrook Press, 2002), 330.

11. Lewis, *The Great Divorce*, chapter 5.

12. Michael Coren, *The Man Who Created Narnia* (Grand Rapids, Mich.: William B. Eerdmans Publishing Company, 1996), 67–68.

13. Dabney Adams Hart, *Through the Open Door: A New Look at C. S. Lewis* (Tuscaloosa: The University of Alabama Press, 1984), 77.

14. Lewis, *Surprised by Joy*, chapter 9.

15. Lewis, *The Great Divorce*, chapter 9.

16. Martindale and Root, *The Quotable Lewis*, 587.

17. Ibid., 587.

18. Ibid., 340.

19. Ibid., 339.

20. Ibid., 345.

21. Wichita State University Department of Mathematics and Statistics, "Logic," http://www.math.wichita.edu/history/topics/logic.html.

22. Keith Devlin, "Math Guy: The Birthday Problem," *NPR* (March 19, 2005), http://www.npr.org/templates/story/story.php?storyId=4542341.

23. Dr. Christopher Mitchell of the Marion E. Wade Center at Wheaton College, Illinois; as quoted in *The Magic Never Ends*, 180.

24. Martindale and Root, *The Quotable Lewis*, 55.

25. C. S. Lewis, *The Four Loves*, from *A C. S. Lewis Treasury* (New York: Harcourt Brace & Company, 1988), 85.

26. Martindale and Root, *The Quotable Lewis*, 55.

27. Ibid., 430.

28. Kenda Creasy Dean and Ron Foster, *The Godbearing Life: The Art of Soul Tending for Youth Ministry* (Nashville: Upper Room Books, 1998), 15.

29. Lewis, *The Great Divorce*, 33.

30. Oswald Chambers, *My Utmost for His Highest* (Westwood, N.J.: Barbour and Company, Inc., 1963), 344.

31. Martindale and Root, *The Quotable Lewis*, 125.

32. C. S. Lewis, *The Lion, the Witch and the Wardrobe* (New York: Macmillan Publishing Co., 1950), 138.

33. Martindale and Root, *The Quotable Lewis*, 287.

34. Ibid., 182–86, 297–98.

35. Colin Manlove, as quoted in *The Magic Never Ends*, 122.

36. Martindale and Root, *The Quotable Lewis*, 246.

37. Paul F. Ford, *Companion to Narnia* (New York: HarperCollins, 1994), 255.

38. James Vlahos, "Disaster on Mount Hood," *National Geographic*, http://www.nationalgeographic.com/ adventure/0208/story.html#story_4.

39. Lewis, *Surprised by Joy*, 197.

40. Duncan, *The Magic Never Ends*, 171–72.

41. Lewis, *The Lion, the Witch and the Wardrobe*, 76.

42. Ibid., 74.

43. Tolkien, *The Tolkien Reader*, 55.

44. Martindale and Root, *The Quotable Lewis*, 399.

45. Ibid., 100.

46. Lyle W. Dorsett, ed., *The Essential Lewis* (New York: Macmillan Publishing Company, 1988), 299.

47. Lewis, *Surprised by Joy*, 225.

48. Sheldon Vanauken, *A Severe Mercy* (New York: HarperCollins, 1980), 93.

49. Martindale and Root, *The Quotable Lewis*, 406.

50. Ibid., 522.

51. Kathryn Lindskoog, *Journey Into Narnia* (Pasadena, Calif.: Hope Publishing House, 1998), 193–94.

52. C. S. Lewis, "Modern Translations of the Bible," from *God in the Dock*, 230, paragraph 2.

53. Chambers, *My Utmost for His Highest*, 209.

54. C. S. Lewis, *Mere Christianity* (New York: Macmillan Publishing Company, 1952), 169.

55. Ford, *Companion to Narnia*, 63.

56. James Martin, "Narni: Journey to the Center of Italy," http://goeurope.about.com/cs/italy/p/narni_italy.htm.

57. Humphrey Carpenter, ed., *The Letters of J. R. R. Tolkien* (New York: Houghton Mifflin Company, 1981), 303, 362, 366.

58. Ibid., 378.

fiction.

Sierra's Story 0-8423-8726-9
Ryun's Story 1-4143-0003-4
Kenzie's Story 1-4143-0002-6

Kyra's Story 0-8423-8284-4
Miranda's Story 0-8423-8283-6
Tyrone's Story 0-8423-8285-2

THE LAMB AMONG ———— THE STARS SERIES

The Shadow at Evening 1-4143-0067-0
The Power of the Night 1-4143-0068-9

other thirsty[?] fiction

Love Rules 0-8423-8727-7
Dear Baby Girl 1-4143-0093-X

nonfiction.

areUthirsty.com

WonkaMania 1-4143-0546-X

The Way I See It 0-8423-0491-6

SHE Teen 1-4143-0028-X

from
Sarah Arthur:

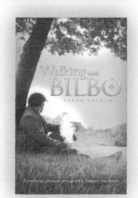

Walking with Frodo 0-8423-8554-1

Walking with Bilbo 1-4143-0131-6

Dating Mr. Darcy 1-4143-0132-4

tap into life.

areUthirsty.com

well . . . are you?

areUthirsty.com

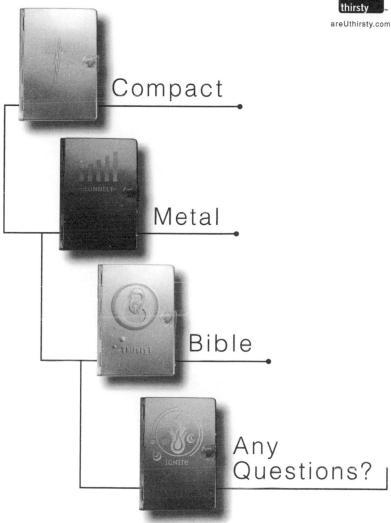

Compact

Metal

Bible

Any
Questions?

Available wherever Bibles are sold